T0354458

Endorsements

Reading these words of Donna's testimony will be a great encouragement to you. Her stories share the path Jesus took her on to become an overcomer. She has opened up her life to encourage you in faith that Jesus will personally take you on a path to your own victories. Beyond this book, she continues to live her life out in victory by the word of her testimony.

—Eugene Wilkerson, pastor
Flames of Fire Ministry
Tacoma, Washington

I met Donna in November 2011. She was asked to join the ministry team at Flames of Fire in Tacoma within six weeks. I ministered by her side for eighteen months and saw her heart for the broken and hurting. Her spiritual gifts from the Lord are effectively used as she pours out the wisdom and understanding that God has poured into her. Donna is genuine in all she says and does.

As she shared her history and life with me, I became excited in how God had worked clearly and powerfully in her life's circumstances. I personally witnessed the move of God in her life.

I highly recommend that those who read this book take the time to study the presence and influence of the Holy Spirit as He restored her life day by day and year by year.

God's personal touch is evident in her life and business. I know that your heart will be changed and challenged as you read her testimonies.

From my experience as her husband of almost four years, I can say that Donna is a fully devoted follower of Jesus Christ. She ministers from a heart of experience.

—Ernest W. Hopper, associate pastor
Flames of Fire Ministry
Tacoma, Washington

What a precious and humbling gift God has given me to work so intimately with Donna on this priceless manuscript; her testimony of the touch of God in her life is up close and real. I love how her personality, emotions, and transparency are expressed. May I forewarn you as you read—your heart will become profoundly moved and aware of the presence of the Spirit of God. Donna is passionate that He is glorified in every detail, which you will witness as each story unfolds before you. May you be encouraged as you read to release the inner lock on your heart. Surrender the key to Jesus, allowing Him to personally touch you for healing, freedom, and peace as He has done for Donna. This is His deepest desire for all of us. Even if our faith is as small as a mustard seed, nothing is impossible for God!

—Rosemary Hosey, editor

Donna has described the lessons learned over her lifetime as a "rich storehouse" to draw from as she ministers to others. Her spiritual memoir offers the same abundant supply to her readers as she tells story after story of her need being met by God's riches. She shows us how to deal with those times when our souls cry out, "How could this happen, Lord?" Over and over again, she has turned to Him in her need, and He has answered. Sometimes through everyday means, other times He met her miraculously. The most beautiful thing of all is that she reminds us that the same God who showed such tender concern for her also longs to do the same for each of us. Reading her book made me want more of Jesus. This book is a page-turner; it was hard for me to put it down.

—Linda Nichols, author of four contemporary Christian fiction books

---

This beautiful book is unlike any other book I have read. This is a personal account of Donna's journey in life as a follower of Jesus Christ. I have known Donna for over thirty years and have witnessed many of these stories as they unfolded. I am amazed at her honesty, wisdom, courage, and determination to find a good lesson in every part of her life. She trusted God even in the thick of trial and crisis.

Through Donna's own personal reflections, this book will help guide the reader through their own journey. Whether joy or sadness, loss or gain, the reader will see that someone else has walked in their shoes!

—Denise Geesey, children's pastor/missionary
US Missions of the Assemblies of God

My friendship with Donna spans over a forty-year period. We shared many seasons of our lives, and we created a strong bond. But Jesus was the real glue of our friendship. She is incredibly open, honest, funny, and passionate about Jesus. I have gleaned deep spiritual truths from her, and we have had many belly laughs as well as shared heartbreaking sorrows over these decades. Although life took us different directions geographically, we have always been amazed at the similar paths of learning the Holy Spirit has taken us on. If I ever was a teacher to her, the role has been reversed many times, as her story has taught me much and continues to do so to this day.

May you see the real Jesus as you read this book! Jesus is relevant. Jesus was the great storyteller. May the Holy Spirit enrich and confirm His work in your life as you read Donna's stories. This is about the transforming gospel of Jesus, the deep teaching and healing power of the Holy Spirit through life events, and how our heavenly Father tenderly loves and cares for us, no matter what life brings our way.

Blessings to you as you read this book. May the real Jesus please stand up in your life!

—Claudia Ussery

THE SCENT

OF MY

TESTIMONY

Donna Gurth Hopper

WESTBOW
PRESS®
A DIVISION OF THOMAS NELSON
& ZONDERVAN

Scripture taken from the New King James Version®. Copyright © 1982 by Thomas Nelson. Used by permission. All rights reserved. Scripture quotations marked (AMP) are taken from the Amplified Bible, Copyright © 1954, 1958, 1962, 1964, 1965, 1987 by The Lockman Foundation. Used by permission. Scripture quotations marked (TLB) are taken from The Living Bible copyright © 1971. Used by permission of Tyndale House Publishers, Inc., Carol Stream, Illinois 60188. All rights reserved.

This book is a work of non-fiction. Unless otherwise noted, the author and the publisher make no explicit guarantees as to the accuracy of the information contained in this book and in some cases, names of people and places have been altered to protect their privacy.

WestBow Press books may be ordered through booksellers or by contacting:

WestBow Press
A Division of Thomas Nelson & Zondervan
1663 Liberty Drive
Bloomington, IN 47403
www.westbowpress.com
1 (866) 928-1240

Because of the dynamic nature of the Internet, any web addresses or links contained in this book may have changed since publication and may no longer be valid. The views expressed in this work are solely those of the author and do not necessarily reflect the views of the publisher, and the publisher hereby disclaims any responsibility for them.

Any people depicted in stock imagery provided by Thinkstock are models, and such images are being used for illustrative purposes only. Certain stock imagery © Thinkstock.

ISBN: 978-1-5127-9994-1 (sc)
ISBN: 978-1-5127-9995-8 (hc)
ISBN: 978-1-5127-9993-4 (e)

Library of Congress Control Number: 2017913530

Print information available on the last page.

WestBow Press rev. date: 09/13/2017

"Remember the former things of old,
For I am God, and there is no other;
I am God, and there is none like Me,
Declaring the end from the beginning,
And from ancient times things that are not yet done,
Saying, 'My counsel shall stand,
And I will do all My pleasure,'
Calling a bird of prey from the east,
The man who executes My counsel, from a far country.
Indeed I have spoken it;
I will also bring it to pass.
I have purposed it;
I will also do it."

—Isaiah 46:9–11 (NKJV)

To the glory of the one true living God,
the Creator of heaven and earth.
You orchestrated each event of my testimony with great care.
I will forever sing Your praises!

"Drink deeply of the scent of this orange carnation, Donna.
Do you see how I have detailed each petal to fit inside the other?
I am going to detail your life as I have detailed this flower,
and the scent of your testimony
will be a sweet-smelling fragrance to my nostrils."

—Anchorage, Alaska 1979

PREFACE

This is the story of one person who thought she was very insignificant. She thought she was too broken to be good for anyone or anything. She felt wasted and destroyed. Hopelessness filled her heart, and there seemed to be no way out. Suffering from depression and perceived rejection, she began to consider suicide. The shame and condemnation she felt were like a heavy backpack she could never put down, but the gospel of Jesus Christ was preached to her as a young child. Seeds were planted that started to sprout inside of her soul and grow her into the person she always wanted to be. It was the love of God and the person of Jesus Christ who rescued her. The Creator Himself was about to recreate her.

This is a compilation of testimonies and stories of how God released her from this burden and changed her from the inside out. His power and His love poured out on her for many years as He taught, guided, and corrected her. He used her daily life experiences to reveal who He really was. Luke 19:10 (NKJV) says it well: "For the Son of Man has come to seek and to save that which was lost."

I am this person, and my name is Donna. This book contains my story, a personal testimony that cannot be argued away. I am both excited and honored to share it with you. The sense of joy and hope God has given to me through the years is the best gift I could have ever hoped to receive. The most important *thing* in my life is not a *thing* but a person. The truth is I have found the Pearl of Great Price, Jesus Christ.

There is no end to this book because I am still very much alive and excited to see all that God still has for me as the future opens up before me. So, sit back with a cup of hot tea, get some tissue, and enjoy! Let the Holy Spirit speak to you through my testimony because He has so much for you as well!

Note: I will be using the names God, Lord, Jesus, and Holy Spirit as I tell my story. They are synonymous in meaning and are part of my vocabulary in attributing honor and glory to the source of my strength. Names of individuals have been changed to honor their privacy.

INTRODUCTION

The birth of this book has been a long time coming. For years, I have felt the birth pangs; I am pressing toward my goal to write it down in obedience to the Lord.

It seems every time I turn around, someone is asking me, "Donna, when are you going to write your book?" Most of these folks have no idea I have been sitting on this for a long time. I have learned the valuable lesson called "no peace, no go" and have been waiting for God's prompting. I did not want to go forward without knowing Jesus was right beside me. It had to be his power, not mine.

Now is the time, and I am stepping out on the edge of a place I have never been before. I am waiting, searching, and yearning for the right words, the right *vision* of how the Lord wants this book to take form. My lack of training as an author is showing like a facial scar. To say that I am a bit timid is an understatement!

A close family member once told me that God had never spoken to him and He would not speak to me either. The person also said that I had no right to tell God anything. I respectfully and completely disagreed with this perspective. I did not reply to these comments. But inside my heart and mind, I knew these comments were a reflection of the person's beliefs, and I was sad for them.

We are talking about the Creator of the heavens and the earth, and if He wants to speak to me, then I want to hear what He has to say! And if I want to tell God something, then it is my privilege as His daughter to do so. Had God not interrupted my thoughts and spoken to me, I am sure my life would not have been restored. God loves to interact with His people. Some listen, and some do not.

Many Christians may not know how to hear the voice of God. There are three voices that speak into our minds. One is the voice of our own mind with its clear, strong thoughts. Another voice is one that brings condemnation, anger, fear, doubt, confusion, and every other strong, dark impression. That voice is always from the kingdom of evil supernaturalism. Satan is the accuser according to the Word of God. I have learned to recognize his voice, take authority over it and submit myself to God. The third voice is the Holy Spirit. He loves to be involved with us, speaking through our spirit into our thoughts. He brings peace with His presence, and His words never contradict scripture. Sometimes He will bring a dream or vision to give direction and deepen the truth of what He is guiding us through. We see this in the Bible frequently.

Jesus said, "My sheep hear My voice, and I know them, and they follow Me" (John 10:27 NKJV). God can speak to us any way He desires. In my experience, I have heard a voice that was audible to me only, loud and strong, full of authority and love. Other times it comes with a deep, sweet impression that will not relent until I obey. There have been times when I was awakened by a gentle stirring in my heart because the Holy Spirit wanted to speak to me about a coming event or even to bring correction to me. He is God, and as I've shared before, I want to hear what He has to say to me!

I hope my story will bless and encourage you. My desire is for you to know more about God during your lifetime on this earth. I have lived these testimonies not only for myself but for those who want hope in their troubled lives. This adventure of learning to trust Jesus, the Son of God, is not just for me; it is for you too!

I understand that many of the people who read this book will disagree with what I am about to share. I encourage you to have an open mind and heart and to keep reading. A true experience with God speaks greater truth than an argument. I did not go looking for these testimonies; they came to me, special delivery from my Creator!

This verse from Psalm 40:1–3 (NKJV) says it so well:

> I waited patiently for the Lord; And He inclined to me, And heard my cry. He also brought me up out of a horrible pit, Out of the miry clay, And set my feet on a rock, And established my steps. He has put a new song in my mouth—Praise to our God; Many will see it and fear, And will trust in the Lord.

ACKNOWLEDGMENTS

I want to say thank you to my husband and sweetheart, Bud, for his consistent encouragement as I wrote my testimony. He would hear me laughing in the office and come running in to enjoy yet another story as God reminded me of the past. I love and cherish you! You are a precious gift from God.

I also want to say thank you to my children, Martin David and Sarah Joy. You have been with me on my life journey and experienced these testimonies. I have shared most of them with you as they happened so that you too could see and understand the love of Jesus Christ. I know He has impacted your lives as He has changed and restored your momma! I love you guys! And to Sheri Lyn, my daughter-in-law, you are also allowing Jesus to restore you, and I'm thankful to call you mine!

To all of the ministry team members who work with my husband and me, you kept after me to get my stories down on paper. I thank all of you! Together we are embracing the calling of God to teach, heal, and deliver in the mighty name of Jesus Christ.

And to everyone who God has used in each story, what a journey we have been on! Some of you are now in eternity, walking with Jesus on streets of gold. Thank you for being part of my restoration!

And to my friend Rosemary, who gave hours of her time and used her skill to prepare the manuscript. You have been such a blessing! When God told me to show the rough draft to you, only He knew how He would use you to bring this book to life! You are a woman of honor.

I want to thank Susan S. Your prayers over this project and encouragement to me have been a blessing. I appreciate you so much. You are a woman of honor.

CHAPTER 1

I SURE WISH I KNEW GOD LIKE THAT!

My life as a child and teenager was filled with continual changes. My dad's job transferred him back and forth from Alaska to Washington State four times. We lived in eleven houses during my childhood. I attended several schools, even spending my fifth grade divided between three different schools.

Wherever we lived, it was very important to my parents to have us in church as much as possible. We normally arrived a half hour beforehand and stayed an hour after the service was over. Every year at our church summer camp, I would make a profession of faith in Jesus Christ and *feel* really good for a short while. But time moved forward, and those feelings would fade in the daily grind of my life.

Because I grew up in church, I developed many ideas of what it meant to be a good Christian. I knew church—knew all the right words to say and was always busy with church activities—but that was about it. I met people who had something spiritual with Jesus that was very real, but I did not know how to get that for myself.

I had an unseen enemy that I had no idea was working behind the scenes of my mind to build a wall between God and me. I did not understand the war Paul talks about in the book of Ephesians.

Satan was laying down a foundation within me. In daily life, I thought I fit in pretty well, but nobody saw the real Donna. Only Jesus saw inside my heart and soul. He had a plan in mind for my life, but I did not know how to access it then.

In our denomination, there was normally a time for testimonies on Sunday nights. I loved hearing all of the stories. They were full of love, joy, and peace. I would spend time at the altar and pray my heart out, feel a bit better, and then go home to the same old Donna once again.

I wanted a testimony in the worst way. I wanted to know God. Slowly the idea began to develop inside my heart that I would just have to listen to others tell their story. I thought I could only get my own if I had been in really terrible sin. I didn't realize my religious pride and my judgmental attitude were just as sinful. I felt cheated out of the relationship with God that other people had.

The darkness inside me was from both the sinful nature I came by at birth and also the bitter roots of anger, fear, and rejection that had already taken hold deep within me from experiences in my young life. I was jealous of just about every one of my friends, and I hated myself. People around me had a tough time with me because I was hard to please, moody, and judgmental. Someone close to me said that I dared people to love me. It was a self-protection move on my part. An event happened in my young life that made me feel absolutely rejected. I was devastated and felt a huge chasm of rejection and anger within me. I am not blaming this person; I am just explaining what was going on within me. It prepared fertile soil for the hopelessness and depression that would engulf me in a few short years.

I was so sensitive to perceived rejection that my emotions were on edge most of the time. It was as if my emotional mind-set thought that everyone was going to reject me; therefore, I interpreted it to be just that. Putting it plainly, I was just a mess!

After graduating from high school, I went to beauty school to become a hair stylist. Now, I had not planned on this being a career; I just figured it was better than nothing. On the advice from a friend, I applied for a scholarship to the local beauty school and won. About six months into it, I realized I could not understand or retain any of the academics required to pass the state exam. I could do the practical stuff really well, but the studies of hair and nail diseases and disorders, and other subjects were way beyond me. I would try to study but to no avail. My mind was so full of anger and fear there was no room for a world full of facts and data. I began to panic as the state boards started approaching.

Then Dad was offered a job transfer to Juneau, Alaska. My parents felt I should move there with them. That was enough to give me the excuse I needed to leave beauty school. Before we left, Dad went to the instructor, canceled my scholarship, and withdrew me. I was relieved and scared at the same time. I hated Alaska and really wanted to stay in my hometown, but I had no skills to provide for myself and no place to live. On the final night in town, I went down to the serene waterfront and made a vow to myself in anger and fear. I determined that I would one day return to live here. From that time on, I never felt settled in any other place. My heart always had a very strong pull back to my hometown.

Upon our arrival in Juneau, I found a job in a small delicatessen down the street from our new church. I worked the night shift and met many new people. One evening, a nice man named Dave came into the store for ice cream. He was a quiet, sweet man, and I felt safe with him. Dave asked me out four times, and I said no. Finally, in conversation, he told me his dad was a minister. On the fifth time asking me out, I said yes.

Now, Dave had a family member who was married with several children. This man had lived in the same town and had a questionable reputation. A few of the ladies in our church had only heard about the other man with the same last name. They did not know about Dave. They attributed to him the reputation of the other man. They brought that juicy bit of gossip to my parents and told them Dave was married and had several children. My parents believed the story because, after all, we were new in town and these were church ladies! No amount of talk would convince them of Dave's single status. I was not allowed to speak his name in their home where I still lived. I knew my parents were hoping I would break up with him, even though they had never met him. Fear fueled their perception of who he was. It was all a smokescreen of deception.

Needing time to think and room to breathe, I quit my job and returned to my hometown. I roomed with a friend and found a job. Dave called me daily, and we would talk about our situation. We decided I should return, and we would face the heat together. Dave bought me an engagement ring, and we set the date to be married. We planned the wedding alone on a shoestring budget. A friend from work made my gown. Being the man of honor that he was Dave went into my Dads workplace and told him we were to be married. He tried to sooth the doubts but my dad was still refusing to walk me down the aisle. Dave and I knew we stood alone but were determined to build a home and a future.

It took an intervention from the pastor of our church to convince my parents that Dave was genuine in his faith and that he was not married. He told them Dave had been coming to the church office for spiritual counsel. Four days before our wedding, Dad agreed to give me away. On April 23, 1973, I became Mrs. David Gurth. We began our life together in Juneau. Our entertainment was to go fishing, find garage sales, and attend the local auction to search for items to furnish our tiny apartment. It did not take us long to decide to leave that small town and move to Anchorage. We both wanted a fresh beginning.

I began to feel a heavy darkness in and over me. I cried so easily; hopelessness pressed in on me as well. My depression only deepened as time passed, and I felt as if I was about to fall over the edge. Dave decided maybe we needed to go visit his parents in Juneau for a few days. While we were there, I asked Dave if we could drive out to a little tourist area called the Shrine of St. Therese. This is a quaint little place built on a small island. A tiny chapel was there, nestled in the trees. Now, I was not Catholic, but that didn't matter; at that point, this quiet place was private enough for me. I asked my husband to wait outside, and I went in and found a seat up front. I felt like I had some serious business to do, but it was only between God and me.

Sitting on the front bench, I looked up to Jesus's image still hanging on the cross. I had heard about Him my entire life but did not really know Him. From the bottom of my heart, I asked Jesus to please do something with my life because I was a mess and I didn't know how to fix myself. I told Him if He didn't want me, then I was going to end my life. I felt cold and dead within. Then a spiritual transaction happened inside of me at that moment. I felt lighter inside and somehow cleaner. The Holy Spirit lifted off of my heart all the burden of my sins, and I knew I had become God's daughter.

Upon returning to Anchorage, we got busy once again with work, household responsibilities, and church activities. I did not read my Bible or pray very much, but I was feeling more at peace.

PERSONAL REFLECTION

I am so thankful to have made that decision long ago, for I had no idea the effect it would have on my family and me for eternity. I had actually entered a whole new realm—God's wonderful kingdom.

Thirty years later, I returned to Juneau when my mother-in-law, Ruth, died. I decided to take a drive out to the Shrine of St.

Therese. Being sentimental, I wanted to say thank you to God in that exact spot. Unfortunately, the building was closed for repairs. So I found a private area to look out over the water and gave thanks to the Lord. It was icy cold, but my tears felt hot on my cheeks as I poured out my feelings from such a different heart than the first time I met God there. Now I had a heart healed and restored. I spoke at Ruth's funeral and had a chance to see the church ladies who had gossiped about Dave many years before. I found that my heart had changed toward them, and all I felt was compassion and love. That is the work of God in me!

Being confident of this very thing, that
He who has begun a good work
in you will complete it until the day of Jesus Christ.
—Philippians 1:6 (NKVJ)

David and Donna Gurth's wedding day

CHAPTER 2

A NEW BEGINNING

Sitting in a movie theater in Anchorage, Alaska, my husband and I were among a very small group of people watching *Across the Great Divide*. I was anxious because this was the first movie I had ever seen, and I was certain if Jesus were to return in the rapture, He would surely go back to heaven without me. This had to be a sin because that is what I had learned as a child. I had many rules embedded in my mind regarding how a Christian should act; I was a cultured Christian, raised with rules and head knowledge, but I had no intimate daily relationship with Jesus Christ.

I felt lost and all alone. I wished I could be like other people. I still had not developed personal devotions at this point, so fear still ruled within me. I was still locked in old thinking patterns, and I felt trapped because I was afraid to live life. I had no idea of the power of God's Word, the Bible. My mind was unchanged even if my spirit was saved. I was sure I would go to hell if I didn't do everything just right. I did not know how to make simple decisions, and everything was a major ordeal. I looked over the fence at everyone else and wished I could fill this inner void. I was ignoring my Bible, just coasting along.

My husband was a new Christian. I had heard about his conversion and knew he was sincere. His joy in his new walk with

7

God and his gladness in being forgiven of sin seemed strange to me. The truth was I envied his ability to just breathe easily in life. He had a deep contentment that I could not reach. Dave thought he married a strong Christian woman, but the inner Donna was far from strong. This loving man wanted to see this movie, and I had agreed to go as long as he assured me there was no vulgarity in it. Dave's freedom was evident as he enjoyed the evening, but I still felt guilty.

I felt guarded within, holding my breath, waiting for God's ax to fall from heaven and sound the verdict of guilty as charged. About halfway through the movie, I heard in my being a loving, authoritative voice say to me:

"Donna, there are many things we need to change about you." Knowing it was God, without hesitation I answered, "Yes, Lord, one thing at a time, one day at a time." And once again, God spoke and said, "Okay."

God had just crossed the great divide of sin between us and reached out to me! There was no doubt He had spoken to me. I sat there in awe at what had just happened. I reached down and picked up the candy bar wrapper I had dropped on the floor. I looked over at Dave, and he was caught up in the movie, laughing at the scene I had just missed. He had no idea what had occurred beside him. Dave had been praying for me because he had come to realize I didn't know Jesus, that I was only familiar with religious rules. I had told him that I had no joy in my salvation a couple years earlier and he responded that I was probably not saved. He got a nasty look from me for speaking those words. I am sure my husband knew that without the intervening hand of God, our life together would be very difficult.

PERSONAL REFLECTION

Dave's prayer had just been answered, and he didn't even realize it. I never dreamed God would show up in the middle of a movie theater and brand my heart with His mercy. I did not know what a wonderful adventure laid ahead for me. The Lord had chosen me ... searched me out, so to speak. He was beginning a work within me called *sanctification,* meaning He was setting me apart for a particular purpose and cleansing me from all the damage my past had done to me.

I had given my heart to Jesus at the Shrine of St. Therese a couple of years before but did not realize my need for spiritual growth through His Word, the Bible, and prayer. I was on hold like a grape on the vine but not ripening. I was still such an empty person! I had many areas of pain and rivers of suppressed anger inside. I didn't realize my relationship with God went two ways. He would do His part, but I had to do mine too. This was a God-size assignment for sure, and it was much deeper than a candy bar wrapper on the floor.

The Lord surveyed my soul and took an inventory of every layer of me. With one step at a time, the Holy Spirit began to show His love and mercy to me in ways that were personal and detailed, so intimately loving. I couldn't help but fall in love with Him, and trust began to grow deep inside of me. I also began to have an intense desire within my heart to read my Bible.

Where can I go from Your Spirit? Or where
can I flee from Your presence?
If I ascend into heaven, You are there; If I make
my bed in hell, behold, You are there.
If I take the wings of the morning, And dwell
in the uttermost parts of the sea,
Even there Your hand shall lead me, And
Your right hand shall hold me.
—Psalm 139:7–10 (NKJV)

Dear Reader,

In the Bible it says that God refines us like silver, and He desires to give us a new heart. There was so much refining that had to be done in my heart. I was certainly in need of His hand on every area of my being. I could feel the need within me, but I had no idea how to fix myself.

The following stories are true; they are the way God chose to refine and grow me. What He had spoken to me in the theater was true. He saw all that was embedded within my soul, and He had a plan to restore me.

As you read, my prayer is that you will find hope in my testimony, and you will seek out for yourself the priceless treasure of learning to lean on Jesus. God required me to be painfully honest as He exposed my heart to His pure and refining love.

> For the word of the Lord is right, And
> all His work is done in truth.
> —Psalm 33:4 (NKJV)

CHAPTER 3

SURPRISED BY THE POWER OF GOD

With this newfound hunger for the Word, I started reading my Bible, and it was finally making sense to me. The Holy Spirit unleashed a great torrent of tears deeply locked inside of me. I would sit on the floor in the corner of our bedroom hugging my Bible—crying, reading, praying, and confessing. The Holy Spirit was opening my soul to the healing hand of Jesus.

I decided to go with a friend to a Bible study in a private home. I really loved both of the ladies who were leading the study. Kay and Norma were real, transparent, and full of God's love. They seemed to genuinely like me. As Kay prayed with my friend, I was standing behind her. Suddenly I felt a flash of electricity go up my arms, and, as if in slow motion, I landed on the living room floor. Waves of warm love washed over me. I cried and laughed at the same time. I had never experienced anything so good, so real, and pure in my whole life. It felt as if God was washing me from within. I could hardly contain the joy. I went home that evening and was in awe as I told my husband what happened.

The next day, I walked into the local grocery store and sensed the prompting of the Lord to walk over to the flowers. Once again, I heard His voice speak to me:

"Drink deeply of the scent of this orange carnation, Donna. Look at how I have detailed each petal to fit into the other. Do you see how beautifully I have detailed this flower? I am going to detail your life as I have detailed this flower, and the scent of your testimony will be a sweet-smelling fragrance to My nostrils."

Deep into my soul poured a gushing love and excitement. I had to leave the store before I lost my composure. I sat in our old car, snow falling, the cold of the Alaskan winter around me, and I wept because of the joy and love that had just been poured out upon my spirit. I had no idea what details the Lord was talking about. I was completely enthralled with the realization that God loved me so thoroughly and He was concerned with my life. I needed hope, and Jesus knew it.

Somehow I felt it was all up to me to make that change inside of me, but God was beginning to get the truth across to me that it was His work within me, and it was also His timing. I began to realize how very close He was in a very personal way. I also was starting to wrap my mind around the reality that He knew when I was going to the grocery store, and He didn't have a problem meeting me there. And I sensed the humor in how God was going to deal with me. I became very aware that He was with me constantly. It was a warm, wonderful feeling to know I could rest in His love.

PERSONAL REFLECTION

As I look back over these events, I am in awe at how the Lord has fulfilled His promise. Cut flowers in the grocery store in the winter do not have a fragrance like that carnation. The scent was strongly sweet and addicting. I believe God touched that particular flower just for me and returned its natural fragrance. I had never smelled the scent of a carnation so strongly or noticed its intricate design and detail.

I didn't comprehend there was so much work to be done in me. I also didn't know how much time would go by as the Lord patiently worked on detailing my life. I was one very impatient woman at times and gave up on myself so often. The Lord has never given up on me, and He never will. This is only one of the many awesome facets of God's divine perspective.

We don't see the entire picture when an artist begins to paint or see the finished pot as the potter molds the clay. The Lord began to work me as clay and to detail the testimony He said would be sweet to Him one day. Like the bulb of a flower, He started to implant faith in Him as my core root. God gave me several encounters with Him to teach me I could trust Him fully. I was not watching for all the details and was not always aware that this was what God was doing as my life unfolded. Through the coming years, I would reflect on the experience in the grocery store, but I was unable to reason it out.

For I know the thoughts that I think toward you, says the Lord,
thoughts of peace and not of evil, to give you a future and a hope.
—Jeremiah 29:11 (NKJV)

He has put a new song in my mouth—Praise to our God;
Many will see it and fear, And will trust in the Lord.
—Psalm 40:3 (NKJV)

CHAPTER 4

AN EMPTY CUP

I wanted to be like my friend Heather in the worst way; she was everything I was not. Her house was pristine; her husband's socks were lined up according to colors. Everything from the outside appearance was what I wanted to be like. I had a bad case of admiration for her. I felt being her friend gave me validity.

Early one morning, I heard sirens screaming in the distance. I learned within a few hours that Heather, her husband, and their two little girls were in a terrible accident caused by a drunk driver. Heather was pregnant with a son and went into labor at the scene of the accident. I wanted to rush to her side and help her. How dare anyone hurt my friend! I went to visit them at the hospital and found this precious couple in the neonatal unit. Luke was caressing his son's tiny head; Heather was stroking his chest. They were telling him of their love for him. Both Mom and Dad were injured. All this pain and suffering made me angry!

I hated death! It had stolen both my grandmothers and a dear friend when she was only eighteen. She was married and had a four-week-old son. Loss and sorrow engulfed me with each death, and I was mad at God. Now I couldn't figure out why my sweet friend was suffering. I prayed in desperation, striving to get God's attention, but it seemed He was out to lunch somewhere. Within a few days, Luke and Heather's precious son, Thomas, died. I did not understand. They were so faithful, so committed to each other and to their church.

When I received the news, I cried with so much deep, heartfelt sorrow. Then I decided I was going to go see Heather to comfort her. I arrived at the hospital with flowers, a card and all the courage I could muster. As I walked into her room, I was overwhelmed by such a tangible peace. The presence of God filled every corner of that space. Heather sat in her hospital bed comforting everyone who showed up. I was amazed by the peace and joy I felt. As I drove home, I made a decision. I just had to know this Prince of Peace who Luke and Heather walked with in a much deeper way.

PERSONAL REFLECTION

I felt undone by this experience. Lacking the ability to give comfort, I was an empty cup wishing I was full. I didn't want to be full of just anything. I wanted to be full of God like Luke and Heather! God brought them a special gift, showing His overwhelming love for them. This special gift came from a lady from our church. She was directed by the Lord several months before the accident to paint a picture. God guided her as she painted, and He told her that He would show her when and to whom she was to give it.

The night Thomas died, Luke stepped out onto the porch and looked up into the sky. He saw a remarkable display of the northern lights. The colors were extraordinary and were seen all down the West Coast. As Luke gazed straight up into the center of the lights, he saw Jesus, and in His arms, He held little Thomas. Across town the Lord spoke to the artist and told her the picture she painted was for Luke and Heather and to name the picture *Beyond This Valley*. The picture was of the northern lights and was a gift of love from the God they trusted. She came over to their home and presented it to them. The picture would hang on their wall as a memorial of Thomas and of God's great love and care.

Heather and I both grew stronger in our faith through this experience. God would use each of us in various ways as we learned that He alone is our source of strength and comfort. I took my eyes off of my friend and put them on Jesus, the Prince of Peace. And that is where my eyes needed to be in the first place. Many years would pass, and eventually Luke and Heather moved to Washington. We rekindled our friendship. It has been exciting to see how God has grown each of us through the years.

> O Lord, You are the portion of my inheritance
> and my cup; You maintain my lot.
> —Psalm 16:5 (NKJV)

CHAPTER 5

A NEW ATTITUDE AND NEW POWER SOURCE

Our son Martin was three years old, and I was doing some daycare in our home to help pad the budget. Dave worked for the US Postal Service, a job that was such an answer to prayer and desperately needed. We had only a single-family car, an old white station wagon that was on its last leg. He came home from work the night before, went to bed, and was sleeping soundly.

I needed to go to the grocery store and tried to start the car, but the battery was dead. Dave woke up and tried to start the car too but to no avail. He hooked up the battery charger, and we waited several hours for it to charge. Later, he returned to find the battery was still dead. Being frustrated, we unplugged the battery charger and put it away. No words were spoken as we walked together into the house.

Our family had no other source of transportation for Dave to go to work, and now we were desperate for help. In my devotion time, I was reading about God's faithfulness to His children and was learning to step out a little at a time to apply faith to the needs of our life. At the prompting of the Lord, we anointed the car hood with oil and prayed over it. The fear and unbelief in us was evident. We turned around and went into the house once again. Not knowing what to do next, I began to vacuum the floor. After about twenty minutes, the Lord said to me, "Now that you've prayed, go outside and start the car." I repeated to Dave what the Lord had said, and we obeyed. Dave inserted the key, and the engine turned over as if it was a brand-new car!

PERSONAL REFLECTION

Our joy knew no bounds. I was jumping around outside like a crazy woman. I think Dave was embarrassed by my loud display, but I did not care. Our faith in God grew by giant leaps that day. God was growing us closer in our relationship to each other and most of all to Him as our loving and ever-present Lord.

Cast your burdens on the Lord, And He shall sustain you;
He shall never permit the righteous to be moved.
—Psalm 55:22 (NKJV)

CHAPTER 6

ANGELS ON DUTY

Our son Martin and his friend Billy loved playing in the dirt pile with their trucks. This particular day, the two of them were outside by the kitchen door, and I was making their lunch. I suddenly heard a loud command from the Holy Spirit to go get the boys *now*! It was so loud and very urgent, and I immediately obeyed and brought the boys inside. As I began to wash them up for lunch, I heard a loud crash and felt a hard thump against the outside wall of our duplex. I went out to check. A car that had been parked at an incline up the hill had come out of gear and rolled down the hill, hitting the back of my car. My car then hit the wall exactly where the boys were playing five minutes earlier.

PERSONAL REFLECTION

God truly has given His angels charge over us! I was driven into quiet worship that afternoon as the boys took their naps. Had God not warned me, had I not obeyed—the consequences were too awful to imagine. God cares about us with the deepest affection and watches over us very carefully.

> For He shall give His angels charge over
> you, To keep you in all your ways.
> —Psalm 91:11 (NKJV)

CHAPTER 7

PROVISION FOR AN URGENT NEED

Later that same year, we were in a financial need. It was the middle of winter, and we needed gas money for Dave to get to and from work at the post office. Dave prayed on his way to work and left the problem with the Lord. The gas tank would run dry that night. He pulled into the large postal employee parking lot, turned off the car, stepped out, and locked the door. As he turned to walk into the building, he looked down to the ground. There, between his feet, was an ice-encrusted twenty-dollar bill! With only his keys to help him, Dave began to poke at the ice until he had freed the twenty-dollar bill. He knew God had kept it safe in the ice just for him. He laid it on the seat of the car to dry and paused to give a heartfelt thanks to the Lord.

PERSONAL REFLECTION

In the many details of our lives as Christians, we need a continual reminder that we are not the ones in control. The Lord alone knows the details ahead for each of us, and He knows just when to enter the scene in a dramatic way. This provision would encourage us in the years to come, reminding us of just how close and attentive our God is. He was building faith in our hearts, and we could feel it growing.

> Call to Me, and I will answer you, and show you great
> and mighty things, which you do not know.
> —Jeremiah 33:3 (NKJV)

CHAPTER 8

RACHEL'S BABY—GETTING UNHOOKED FROM SOAP OPERAS

When I was a young mother, I became addicted to TV soap operas. I would make sure my son was very tired for his afternoon nap so I could watch my shows undisturbed. This addiction was having a negative effect on my emotions, and I didn't see it, but the Lord did, and He used a rather humorous way of getting my attention.

The story line of my favorite one reads like this: It was cliffhanger Friday, and Rachel was in labor! As viewers, we had waited so long for her to conceive, and then we wondered if Max, her husband, would stay with her through the pregnancy and if he would fall in love with her once again. Alas, Rachel was having her baby, and I sat glued to the screen. I was devastated when the doctor broke the news ... Rachel's baby had died! My own emotions were deeply buried inside. The reality was I had lost several pregnancies to miscarriage and had not dealt with my own pain. It was easier to focus on someone else, even if that person did not exist.

I could not control the wave of emotion that hit me. I cried as if it had been my own baby. I spent the afternoon aching, crying, and mourning over Rachel's baby. When my husband arrived home that evening, I was cooking dinner and still aching from Rachel's loss.

I was making my go-to comfort food ... homemade spaghetti and lots of it. Dave heard me crying and came into the kitchen. Even the smallest show of affection from him was enough to cause my built-up emotions to explode. Dave questioned me, "What's wrong, babe?" Without realizing it, I sobbed out the words, "Rachel lost her baby!" Dave looked at me and asked, "Who is Rachel?"

His question shocked me back into reality, and the Lord used that moment to speak to me. "You have become an emotional basket case because of a woman and a baby that does not exist. Your entire afternoon has been spent in tears and emotional turmoil. Donna, you have not dealt with your own reality and have vented your pain at the feet of a lie. They do not exist, but you do." The Lord brought me to my knees that night.

And Monday was coming! Did Rachel *really* lose the baby? Would Max stay or leave her? I never knew the answers to these questions. I was very busy on purpose the following Monday. I knew I needed to stay away from the television. At this time in my young life, I began making some changes; I played worship music daily, and I chose to live in reality, allowing God the right to enter my world and do a deep cleansing of my emotions.

PERSONAL REFLECTION

This experience and the freedom the Lord brought me into through this taught me how quickly my mind could go off into fantasy thinking and how easily I could become upset by something that was not a reality. I learned I desperately needed to lean on Jesus and not allow any false feelings or emotions to carry me away from the truth. I guess I could say that God plucked one rotten petal from the flower that day so that He could fill that spot with a new one. There was more to come as my future lay before me. God had the inventory of my life before him. I did not. That was a very good thing!

Search me, O God, and know my heart;
Try me, and know my anxieties;
And see if there is any wicked way in me,
And lead me in the way everlasting.
—Psalm 139:23–24 (NKJV)

CHAPTER 9

THE STORY OF MARYANN

We received news that some former acquaintances were moving to town. Without notice, they showed up at our door late one night. We were the only people they knew in town, and they had no food or place to live. Because of unpleasant events that happened in their past, we were very concerned, but we felt compassion for the children and knew they were hungry and tired. For about two years, we helped them as best we could for the sake of the children. There was resistance to any conversation of a relationship with God due to past experiences of abusive and false religious teachings by others. So we prayed for them and continued to do what we felt was right.

One evening, I received a call from the mother, who I will call Maryann. She started talking about how hopeless she felt, and she wanted to end her life. I went to her immediately and also asked two of my friends from church to visit her. Because of the previous resistance we got, I thought that a couple of outside people would have greater acceptance with Maryann. I was right about that decision, and Maryann not only opened up her heart to them, but she received Jesus as her savior and Lord that day. She dearly loved both ladies and told me she never had such real friends before. But Maryann's husband, Jack, was not happy with all this; he was very angry and fearful. We only had a short time to nurture Maryann in her newfound faith. Jack learned that the police were going to arrest him. After quickly selling all their possessions, the family fled town. I was very concerned about Maryann. So Dave and I prayed for her and trusted that God had her in His hands.

A few years later, we received a call from Jack that Maryann was dying in the hospital. I decided to call a minister near them, and he agreed to go see Maryann. We prayed that Jack would not be anywhere nearby so the minister could freely speak to her and pray with her. God answered that prayer! God loved her more than we did. After Maryann passed away, the family once again decided to move back to our town. We had one more chance to love on the grieving children and to encourage Jack. I asked the Lord to please give me some kind of insight that Maryann was all right spiritually and that she was indeed in heaven. I got my answer in the most unusual way.

One afternoon before Dave was due home, Jack came over to our house. It was very hard to have him near us; his rough personality didn't sit well with me. But that day the Lord had a purpose for his visit. It seemed like Jack had been crying, and while sitting in my rocking chair, he began to talk to me about the last day of Maryann's life. Jack excused his tears and cleared his throat, saying, "You know, Donna, I'm not a religious man." He then told me she was not alone in the hospital room. He sensed a loving, calm presence and said it felt like, had she been able talk, she would say, "I am coming home, Lord."

Personal Reflection

Jack didn't realize that God was speaking through him, and assurance filled my heart that Maryann was indeed home in heaven, forever released from her torment. I love how the Holy

Spirit answers our heart's questioning. He is so faithful, and I will never forget how He used a difficult man to bring the answer I needed. My heart was glad that my friend was enjoying the presence of Jesus, and I look forward to our reunion one day.

I will not leave you as orphans (comfortless, desolate,
bereaved, forlorn, helpless); I will come (back) to you..
—John 14:18 (AMP)

CHAPTER 10

GOD THE REALTOR

Renting had become a burden; we desperately wanted our own home and yet knew nothing about the process of searching out a house we could afford. We went to our source, Jesus, and prayed about it. Dave and I looked at many homes we thought we could afford, but becoming discouraged with what we found, we almost gave up. I read an ad in the paper one evening and called on the house only to find out it was already sold. The agent asked me if Dave had used his VA loan yet, and I assured him he had not. After giving him our phone number, the call ended, and it would be another three years before we were to hear from this agent again.

During this waiting season, the Lord was revealing my pride, because I wanted to measure up to all of our friends who had nicer homes. Somehow I thought if we didn't own a bigger and better home, or at least one like theirs, this equaled failure on my part. Keeping up with the material possessions of others was somehow more important to me than keeping to the household budget. It equated with success in my mind, when we looked as good on the outside as our friends. I gave up any idea of owning our own home and began to feel sorry for myself.

Then one day, right out of the blue, the real estate agent called with an opportunity that would take us to the nicest house we had looked at. The seller needed a veteran to take over his loan so he could buy another home. All we needed to do was put down fifty dollars for a credit check. We later learned the sellers were also Christians and had prayed for another Christian couple to buy their home. This opened up an avenue of ministry for Dave and me as we shared the story of God's faithfulness to us with the real estate agent and with the family who sold us their home.

There were many opportunities for us to meet neighbors and talk with them about our testimonies. This house is where I sat in the corner of the bedroom hugging my Bible and praying. Many of my early lessons in learning to trust for God's provision were learned in this house. There is a time and a purpose for every place and every event in our lives. God does not miss one detail.

PERSONAL REFLECTION

Four years later, we were praying to sell this home, and, according to our request, the Lord sent a Christian couple. We were able to bless them with a great deal! The equity helped provide funds for us to relocate to Washington State, a move that God had ordained. Once we had purchased and lived in the house, I realized that a house is just a house. I didn't need to measure up to everyone else. Our true home was each other and Jesus. Peace was in my heart as I learned that the important things are not things but relationships with people, and especially my walk with God.

And my God shall supply all your need according to His riches in glory by Christ Jesus. Philippians 4:19 (NKJV) (NKJV)

CHAPTER 11

My Special Rug

Owning a new home was more of a financial obligation than I had imagined, and money was very tight. I wanted to decorate the house, and one of the things I needed was a kitchen rug. Winter mornings in Alaska can leave a tile floor very cold under your feet. This was in the seventies, so the decor was all done in autumn colors. I visualized a rug in brown, orange, green, and yellow shades. But the money to buy one was not there. I accepted the fact we would just have to put up with the cold kitchen floor, but God saw my heart's desire.

Not too long after deciding to let go of my wish, I found my rug in a most unusual way. Our home was in the outskirts of Anchorage. There were not many neighbors between our house and the grocery store. Then one day as I was driving on this very cold and lonely road to the store, I spotted a lump of something in the middle of the road. Being the curious type, I slowed the car down and looked closely at the lump. Could it be? Well, how about that! It was a kitchen rug just like the one I wanted. I stopped and looked around to see if the owners were nearby. I was alone on that road. The rug had been run over by other cars and was dirty. I was thrilled with my find and took it home and washed it up. It served me well for over six years, keeping our feet warm in the cold Alaskan winters.

PERSONAL REFLECTION

I knew instantly this rug was a gift from God, so personally given as His provision for the seemingly incidental things in my life. I so joyfully accepted it! It doesn't take much for little things to touch a heart hungry for Jesus. The thought that He would care about a small thing like a rug prepared my heart to believe for bigger things that would come in the future.

The funny thing is I was just what He was looking for as well! I was much like this rug; lost, run over, and dirty. Jesus willingly pulled me to Himself, washed my sinful heart with His blood, and made me a part of His eternal family.

I learned early that the Lord was concerned first of all with my heart attitude toward Him and my obedience to His Word. I was very careful to avoid prosperity teachings because I had seen the damage in the lives of many who tried to control God with their prayers and commands. I knew if I chose to obey the Lord and seek Him first of all, then I didn't need to worry about provision. This truth would prove itself out many times as the years passed by. It's like the new doll or truck you got for Christmas as a child. Oh the fun of new things! But in a short time the newness passes and it does not meet the need of the heart. Only Jesus satisfies the soul of the human heart. I was soon to realize how fulfilling it was to wait on the Lord each day. The excitement of answered prayer was thrilling to me. He always gave the answer to me in ways that were beyond what I had expected. Completely God-like and nothing I could have figured out on my own.

But seek first the kingdom of God and His righteousness, and all these things shall be added to you. —Matthew 6:33 (NKJV)

CHAPTER 12

ONE LITTLE BOY, A BIG WHEEL, AND A DREAM

Christmas brought our son Martin a big-wheel bike complete with siren and clacking wheel sounds. He was thrilled with his new toy, and as a four-year-old and a new driver, he had rules to follow. One of our rules stated that the bike would not go out of the driveway for any reason, and before naptime, it would be parked in the backyard. This particular day, Martin forgot, and the bike disappeared during naptime. Martin was crushed, and we were too broke to buy him a new one. Our first step was to pray and ask the Lord to show us where the bike was.

The next morning came, and Dave had the day off. Arising at about eight o'clock, Dave sat straight up in bed and was so excited. He didn't say anything except "Oh." Out the door he went! Martin and I were bewildered by his sudden exit. About thirty minutes later, we had our answer. God gave Dave a dream and revealed exactly where Martin's bike was. In the dream, he saw a specific road in our subdivision and a specific yard with the bike. It took less than five minutes to drive to the house. The child who took the bike was talked into it by his friend on their way home from school the day before. The mother of the child was surprised as

Dave showed her Martin's initials that were carved into it the day it was assembled.

PERSONAL REFLECTION

Now you might be thinking, *Doesn't God have bigger things to worry about? Isn't He holding up the stars and doing other enormous things? Why would such a small thing matter to the Creator of the universe?* I am glad you asked! We are what matters to Him; we are His workmanship, and He cares about every detail that makes us who we are. He knew we were unable to provide a new bike, and so He brought back the old one. The Lord began to show me his desire to be reconciled to every area of my life, even daily things like this.

The Lord sees the future, and He knows just what we need to help us grow in our faith and trust in Him for the times ahead. He knew we needed to see His hand in the small things too. And God foresaw what I would face one day, and I needed a solid faith foundation under me. New petals of trust and awareness of God's presence were budding deeply inside of me.

My sheep hear My voice, and I know them, and they follow Me.
—John 10:27 (NKJV)

CHAPTER 13

MARY'S CRY FOR HELP

One church I attended was located near the downtown area and was frequented by many street people looking for help. One of these individuals was a lady named Mary. Mary began coming into the church, and she would sit in the back row holding her head in her hands. We were very aware of this lady, but it was intimidating to us. It frustrated me that I didn't know how to help her. One Sunday evening, my friend saw Mary standing in the corner of the bathroom talking to the wall in front of her. Suddenly she turned and looked up at my friend and said, "Do you know that I could kill you?"

The following Sunday, Mary sat behind me. I had not spoken to her but was very aware of her presence. At the end of the worship service, she suddenly screamed out, "Whatever that is inside tormenting me, come out in the name of Jesus!" I held my breath, but not one person came to minister to her. I was disappointed, and my heart ached for her. I looked around, hoping to see at least one board member come to her aid, but there was no one. I had heard about demonized people but had never encountered one. Now it was happening right behind me.

I prayed, "Lord, who will help her?" Then the Lord prompted me to reach out to her myself. I remember thinking, *Okay, Lord, here we go!* I turned and asked Mary if she wanted to come with me and I would pray for her. I had no idea what was awaiting me. When we got to the downstairs area, Mary looked at me and said, "Oh, Donna, I didn't know it was you!" The sobering reality was that Mary didn't know me, but the demonic forces within her did. They know every born-again child of God, and they hate our testimonies. I asked Mary if I could touch her, and she said yes. I laid my hand on her shoulder and began to pray, seeking God for guidance and for help. At this point, Mary screamed and ran out the back door of the church.

I began to become physically ill, and my husband took me home. I went to bed and could feel a war going on over my head. I literally felt a spiritual enemy trying to come against me, but the Lord laid down a blanket of protection above me. I was pressed down on the bed and put into a deep sleep as Dave prayed over me. I awoke about two hours later, and the war was over; I was no longer ill. The pastor of my church called me the next day and told me that he wanted me to go with another woman to visit Mary and pray for her. I promptly refused his request. I knew I was not ready to engage in this type of spiritual warfare.

PERSONAL REFLECTION

This was my first encounter with spiritual warfare, and I knew that the Lord had protected me. I never saw Mary again. God uses on-the-job training to begin to prepare us for the future He is leading us into. Today I would never approach this kind of supernatural evil alone. Jesus sent the disciples out two by two, and that's very wise.

We all make choices every day to seek truth and light or to play in the enemy's sandbox and become ensnared with darkness. I've often wondered why Mary became so tormented in her mind. I do not know what happened to her, but Jesus does. He heard her cry for help. He will bring her into freedom; He died on the cross for her too.

> Finally, my brethren, be strong in the Lord
> and in the power of His might.
> Put on the whole armor of God, that you may be
> able to stand against the wiles of the devil.
> For we do not wrestle against flesh and blood,
> but against principalities, against powers,
> against the rulers of the darkness of this age,
> against spiritual hosts of wickedness
> in the heavenly places. Therefore take up the whole armor of God,
> that you may be able to withstand in the evil
> day, and having done all, to stand.
> —Ephesians 6:10–13 (NKJV)

CHAPTER 14

GARAGE SALE MIRACLE

In 1983, we began to feel a strong urge to leave Alaska and move to Washington State. We sold our home and started the process of sorting through our belongings. We temporarily moved into a duplex to wait out the day of our big move out of state. My friend and I decided to have a garage sale. We combined our items and spent the day dickering with buyers. I also had a big pot of navy bean and ham soup on the stove simmering for dinner when Dave arrived home from work. I could have sold several bowls of soup as buyers came and went.

I felt sorry for our new landlord having to rent out our duplex again, and at the same time I was not thrilled with the challenge of selling our king-sized bed. On the final day of our garage sale, I said to my friend, "Wouldn't it be just like God to send someone in here to rent this apartment, buy the king bed, and also everything we have left to sell?" Within a few minutes, a man came in and asked if the duplex was available to rent, did we want to sell our bed, and, by the way, could he buy everything that was left in the garage sale. Good grief! I had been feeling like we were stepping out on thin ice, but this event reminded me that we were on the rock Christ Jesus.

PERSONAL REFLECTION

I worried that we were making a mistake to give up the first
solid job Dave had ever held. I needed to see we were not alone, that
God was with us in this decision. At times, people wear me out with
too many questions, and sometimes I have wondered how God has
put up with me through the years as I have questioned Him at times
about His silence. The truth is He was occasionally silent because
I was misunderstanding His detailed direction over my life. My
prayers were fueled by fear. I didn't have the whole picture, but He
did. Eventually I saw things His way, and that always humbles me.
It still does!

The Lord God has given Me The tongue of the learned, That
I should know how to speak A word in season to him who is
weary. He awakens Me morning by morning, He awakens
My ear to hear as the learned. The Lord God has opened
My ear; And I was not rebellious, Nor did I turn away.
—Isaiah 50:4–5 (NKJV)

CHAPTER 15

READY, SET, GO!

People do mean well, I am sure, but we had so many friends who kept warning us to not leave Alaska. One of my friends at church said something to me that I have never forgotten. She said, "Donna, just because God confirms something to you doesn't mean He will confirm it to other people in your life." True, how true! Dave and I both lived in Alaska most of our lives, but when God started drawing us to move, there was no question about it. We had seen His hand so many times in this, and now we were in the place where staying would feel like disobedience.

We'd sold our chairs, so sitting on the floor was how we spent our evenings waiting for our moving day. I was looking forward to having a garden and canning the produce. I bought a special book on canning and freezing vegetables. I remember sitting on the floor, reading my book cover to cover while Dave and our son, Martin, played Pac-Man on the new Atari. Our move day was fast approaching, and then in the late fall of 1983 we boarded Alaska Airlines to begin a new adventure in the Lower 48.

PERSONAL REFLECTION

There were so many events that were going to happen in our lives in Washington that God wanted us to be out of Alaska and close to family. We fought our own fears and questions as we made this choice to move, but the Holy Spirit confirmed it to us over and over again. It is in these big events of our lives that God reveals who he truly is. We were to experience many more divine appointments in the years to come.

The steps of a good man are ordered of the
Lord, And He delights in his way.
—Psalm 37:23 (NKJV)

CHAPTER 16

LIFE IN WASHINGTON, WE'RE GOING POSTAL!

Our move to Washington in December 1983 had been orchestrated by Jesus, and we felt this would draw us closer as a family. We knew we needed to depend upon Him continually, and as a couple, we were learning to lean on Him day by day. Finding a job was our next big hurdle in trusting Him.

Dave began to search for employment. Taking an impressive letter of recommendation from his supervisor, Mary, my husband applied to several postal stations in the area. One station he refused to apply to was Federal Way. He knew they kept only the best of the best carriers. Dave did not have confidence he could make their ninety-day probation period. One of the stations he also applied to was Auburn, unaware that they did the hiring for Federal Way. Dave got a call from the Auburn Post Office, and they offered him a full-time position. I was so overcome by emotion because he had a job I flopped down on our bed and cried, "Thank you, Jesus!"

Dave looked into the bedroom and said, "You remind me of the children of Israel, 'Oh for the leeks and the garlic of Egypt!'"

"Ouch!"

On his first day of work, he reported to Auburn and was told he would be working out of the Federal Way office. Dave was scared stiff! That was the one place he had refused to put in an application. Years of feeling insecure had taken their toll on his confidence, but God had something to prove to Dave. The first ninety days were tough. Dave's supervisor was going through a hard time in her personal life, and she was venting on the employees. Day after day, he would come home devastated. It seemed as though Lucy had a personal grudge against Dave. At the end of each workday, I would kneel in front of Dave's recliner, and we would pray together and ask God to help Dave and to bless his supervisor.

We decided to apply God's Word to the situation. In Luke 6:27–28(NKJV), we read, "But I say to you who hear: Love your enemies, do good to those who hate you, bless those who curse you, and pray for those who spitefully use you." We chose to pray and wait it out.

Dave's ninety-day probation period came to an end, and Lucy called him into her office. She told him she would give him her decision on Monday. Needless to say, we prayed a lot that weekend. God has a way of thinking ahead, and little did we know He had already taken some extreme measures to work on this decision. What we didn't know was Dave's old supervisor, Mary from Anchorage, had *just happened* to schedule her vacation in Seattle and *just happened* to be at the same party Lucy was attending that very evening. It was not a postal event, and considering the size of Seattle and the whole scope of things, this was a miraculous move of God.

At the party, Mary and Lucy *just happened* to meet and started to talk. As their conversation began to unfold, Dave's name was mentioned. Mary convinced Lucy to give him the benefit of the doubt. Mary said that Dave had been one of her favorite carriers and she missed him. God had arranged this miracle on behalf of two insignificant people in Milton, Washington, who dared to trust Him.

Monday morning brought the revelation from the personnel office that Dave was hired full-time—permanent! On the Friday before, Dave knew he had not made the grade for the job, but God had brought about a *chance* meeting at a party in Seattle that very evening. Dave worked at the Federal Way Post Office for seven years. Eventually he was promoted to become a supervisor. Dave then became Lucy's boss. There were many ministry opportunities for him as he applied himself to his job. He knew God's hand was upon him, and he treated the employees including Lucy with grace and mercy.

PERSONAL REFLECTION

This encounter taught me that regardless of the situation, when the Lord has an appointment for His children, nothing can stop His plan. I was to find a new depth of trust in the Lord through this encounter. God has a sense of humor indeed, and we were to see more and more how He would detail our lives as time went by.

Trust in the Lord with all of your heart, And
lean not on your own understanding;
In all your ways acknowledge Him, And
he shall direct your paths.
—Proverbs 3:5 (NKJV)

CHAPTER 17

TINA'S LAST CHANCE

In 1984, we received a call from a family member in Alaska who asked us to go visit someone who lived near us in an adult care facility.

As Dave and I entered the facility, we saw a sad sight; the conditions were horrid, the home was dirty, and it was evident that they operated with very low standards. We were ushered into a small, damp, and dirty room. Upon introducing ourselves, we tried to strike up a conversation, but Tina and her husband were not interested in our visit. We didn't stay long, but we promised to return with a large-print Bible and more news of the family who had sent us. Dave and I took some of our grocery money, purchased the Bible, and came back to present it to them. We returned months later only to find the Bible on the bottom of a pile of magazines and covered with dust.

One year later, we received another emergency call, and it brought news that Tina was deathly ill and hospitalized. Dave and I promised we would go once again and try to minister to her. We didn't realize what a fight we would have just trying to get to the hospital. It was one obstacle after another—work schedules, no babysitter available, car problems, and road closures. But we finally made our way to St. Joseph's in Tacoma. This was an example of the hindrances believers can encounter as they step out to obey the Lord.

Dave and I entered Tina's room and were shocked to find her drawn up in a fetal position and about fifty pounds thinner. We were told she was in a coma and had not been awake for several days. Looking at the silent form on the bed, Dave and I prayed, asking God to wake her long enough to give her one final chance to make her peace with Him. Dave stood by the door, praying for me as I stepped forward to minister to Tina. As I bent over her bed, she awoke. Her breathing was labored, and I could hear liquid gurgling in her lungs. Her eyes showed that she recognized me.

I asked Tina if she knew me, and she responded by shaking her head. I told her that she was very ill and dying. She nodded her head yes. With boldness from the Holy Spirit, I asked her if she wanted to make peace with God. Once again, she nodded yes. I told her God was looking upon her heart, and if she believed that Jesus was Lord and wanted forgiveness for her sins, that He would be faithful and forgive her. I prayed out loud, and Tina followed my every word.

Tears were flowing down her thin, hollow cheeks as she gave her heart to Jesus. We spent a few moments encouraging her with words of love. The last sound I heard as we left the room was Tina whispering, "Oh, sweet Jesus, thank you." Tina died later that week.

Personal Reflection

God gave us this time with Tina as a gift, and we were shouting victory all the way home! When we arrived home, our neighbor stood and stared at us as we went into our house. We were to find out later that they had seen much more than just Dave and me. We were told that we were literally shining God's presence as we stepped out of the car and went into the house. Our neighbor had friends who were telling them about Jesus, and we had no idea. Seeing us glow that day had given them much to consider. We later learned they gave their lives to the Lord. God used us that day for the sake of Tina and also our neighbor.

When I was standing by Tina's hospital bed, I remember thinking about my own life. I wanted to finish well in Christ, having lived for His glory and to help others. I drove a stake of determination into my soul that day. Only what's done for the kingdom of God has any meaning whatsoever.

> But you, beloved, building yourselves up on your most
> holy faith, praying in the Holy Spirit, keep yourselves in
> the love of God, looking for the mercy of our Lord Jesus
> Christ unto eternal life. And on some have compassion,
> making a distinction; but others save with fear,
> pulling them out of the fire, hating even
> the garment defiled by the flesh.
> —Jude 1:20–23 (NKJV)

CHAPTER 18

MY LONG-DISTANCE PRAYER REQUEST

One day, as I was cleaning house, I heard a radio program called Contact America. This program, based in Washington, DC, was basically about political issues as they related to our Christian faith. Other subjects also covered everyday events, and at times they would open up their phone lines for personal prayer requests.

I was feeling that familiar deep yearning for the baby girl we wanted, but we were having many fertility problems with no answers. On this day, I decided to call Contact America and ask them to pray for us. I told them of the eight miscarriages I had and of our desire for a baby girl. The radio host prayed for us with great compassion. "Bear one another's burdens, and so fulfill the law of Christ" (Galatians 6:2 NKJV). As I hung up, I had no emotions one way or the other. Little did I know that God was about to do a great miracle!

The rest of this chapter tells that story.

THE MIRACLE OF SARAH JOY

It was the evening of April 11, 1974. I was wrapped up in a lovely pink nightgown, but I was not feeling so lovely. I had lost our first baby, and it was also my twenty-second birthday. I returned home from a three-day stay at the local hospital feeling so empty, so brokenhearted. Dave couldn't say any words that would soothe the agony of loss I was feeling. All I had ever dreamed of was being a mother. I was hand-sewing a lovely baby blanket during the first six week of this pregnancy, and now I packed it away. I felt deeply insecure and full of condemnation. Those feelings drove me into more depression. Little did I know I would face this pain many times over as the years would pass by. I would unpack the blanket and work on it only to pack it away once again.

Trips to fertility specialists provided no answers. Medical procedures yielded no hope, and my dream of motherhood would loom in front of me like the impossible dream. I would lose a total of eight babies to miscarriage, each time thinking it was my fault. I did not give any consideration that our miscarriages were the fault of something other than me. I gave up finally and made myself busy with work. In 1977, I had flu symptoms but never gave one thought to being pregnant. Finally, Dave forced me to have a pregnancy test. I forgot about checking on the results and didn't bother to call the family care clinic. They had to call me later in the day with the news that I was indeed pregnant, and according to the test, I was beginning my second trimester.

We were shocked, thrilled, and filled with anticipation. We went for an ultrasound, which confirmed I was almost four months pregnant and the baby was very active. It was a total miracle, a blessing beyond what we expected! God intervened and caught us by surprise. For some reason, I had forgotten about the blanket packed away. Martin David was born on July 27, 1977, and we were in love from the moment we gazed into his sweet face.

The blanket was too feminine for our big boy, so I left it tucked away. After bringing our son home, I slept for twelve straight hours. I awoke to hear Dave crying and got up to see him rocking Martin and cuddling him in his arms. I heard Dave say, "Thank you, Jesus! Oh, thank you, Jesus!" We had so much fun with Martin, adoring this sweet miracle; he was so cute, so bald, and his laugh brought us to tears. As any new parents, we would watch him sleep and denied ourselves some of life's comforts to be sure he had all he needed.

We thought that surely after the birth of our son, the miscarriage problem would end, but it did not. It was tormenting to have no answers. It would be several more years before being told by the Veterans Administration that Dave was poisoned by exposure to over 250,000 gallons of both Agent Orange and Agent White while serving in Vietnam. The VA contacted Dave for a physical exam, and they asked him this question: "Has your wife had a problem with repeated miscarriages?" Caught off guard, there were no words we could speak.

Shortly after this, I saw a Vietnamese family with several children at the grocery store. I felt so jealous and angry. I wanted to yell at them, but I turned around and hurried over to my car instead. I had a prayer meeting between God and me. I repented of my anger and my jealousy. The truth is it was not anyone's fault, and I refused to have this bitterness inside me.

Many of the couples we knew had several children, and our son was wishing he had siblings too. One morning, Martin climbed in bed beside me and said, "Mommy I want a baby sister so bad I can hardly throw up!" Those sweet words were from a true heart within our son. But to me it dug deep, and I replied we were trying to give him a baby sister and asked him to pray to Jesus about his desire.

With the news of each new pregnancy, I would pray and wait, reminding God in my prayers that if He would bless us with a baby girl, I would name her after Sarah in the Bible. After all, He had answered Sarah's prayer in giving her and Abraham the desire of their heart when Isaac was born.

With the eighth and final miscarriage I was admitted to the hospital by my doctor. They put me in a private room in the maternity unit. I was losing my baby and all I could hear in my room was the crying of newborns. For some reason a nurse brought a baby girl into my room and left her right by the side of my bed. I got up and dressed, signed myself out of the hospital against the doctor's wishes and went home. I knew the routine of miscarriage and I could go through it on my own. Lying on our bed at home I began to cry. My words were from a heart full of pain as I questioned why God would let that nurse to put someone else's baby girl by my bed.. Dave held me in his arms as I spoke those bitter words. I decided to stop praying about another baby, packed away the blanket, and tried to put it out of my heart. But God was not ignoring my prayers; He had not forgotten!

After our move from Alaska to Washington in 1983, I began teaching a Bible study at our church. The Lord did His homework well as He prepared me to lead the study, and it began with promise— thirty-six ladies attended our first class. On the very first evening, before the class began, two ladies invited me to a side room in order to pray for me. Laying their hands on me, they began to pray. Suddenly, I felt hot, thick oil being poured over my head. It ran slowly down my entire head and onto my shoulders. The sensation of it was such that I held my breath. Laura, one of the ladies who was praying with me, said, "Donna, I see a pitcher of oil and a hand pouring it over you! You are being anointed for ministry. Do you feel that?" I replied I had been feeling it for almost two minutes before she spoke. I still ponder that experience. I consider it to be a sacred moment to this day. Only God knows what His intention is for my life.

After the second Bible study class, as I was driving home, the Lord spoke to me about the baby girl I wanted. I reminded the

Lord that this subject was one that brought up painful emotions. I didn't want to lose my composure in front of all the ladies at the next study feeling like this. There were two ladies in particular who were intimidating to me, and I was uncomfortable around them. The next week, both those ladies were absent from the study. Just as the Lord loves to do, He changed our Bible study completely that evening and opened up my heart to share my desire for a baby girl and about the past eight miscarriages. With great love and kindness, these wonderful ladies prayed for me for the birth of my baby girl. What they didn't know was my faith was so tiny; even a mustard seed would have been huge in comparison.

In my mind, I was telling God that *if* He had one of these ladies say something about the name "Sarah," then I would know it was okay to conceive again. Ten minutes later, a lady named Karen approached me and said God had spoken to her. She was told to speak to me and say that the name Sarah meant *princess* and she would be a joy to the King of kings. Needless to say, the floor could have opened up and swallowed me, and I would not have felt it!

Several days passed, and one night as I was sitting on the edge of our bed, the Lord spoke to me once again and told me to "get on your face and pray for the life of the child." I did not know it at this point, but I was pregnant again, and Sarah Joy was on the way! I obeyed and prayed until I sensed the release of the burden to pray. Within three weeks, I was very sick. I took a pregnancy test, and it was positive. The ladies at the next study went wild with joy when they heard the news. But I was unable to attend that class; I was at home hugging the toilet. My doctor told me being so sick was a good sign that the hormones were strong and this baby was going to make it.

By the fourth month, I was uneasy. This was always the point when I lost the other babies, and fear kept trying to attack me. My faith was being tested day by day. I was afraid of disappointing the ladies in my Bible study, and I was also feeling somehow responsible that if I lost this baby, their trust in God would be hurt. It's amazing how we think sometimes when we are not mature enough to see the sovereignty of God's hand. It is not up to us to make things happen; God is in control all of the time! On one particular night, I was filled with fear, and I kept getting up to check for bleeding. I was so scared I would miscarry. Only God and I knew what was happening to me through the long hours of the night.

At about five o'clock in the morning, the phone rang. It was Laura from the Bible study. She was awakened by the Lord at 4:00 a.m. and told to call me with a scripture and a word from God to encourage me. Now, I knew Laura wasn't looking in my bedroom window all night. I fully realized this had to be God! The word she gave me was "Relax, Donna," and the scripture was Psalm 121:4 (NKJV), "Behold, He who keeps Israel Shall neither slumber nor sleep." I was special to God. He saw me all night long.

The peace of God flowed over me; I unpacked the baby blanket and started to finish it. God's peace continued until the seventh month when the doctors were becoming concerned with the possibility of birth defects. They knew Dave had been exposed to dioxide poisoning in Vietnam, and this could possibly cause horrid defects in the baby. The test they recommended was an amniocentesis. The risk of the test was miscarriage, and we'd had enough of that. So we told them this was God's baby and we would take her in whatever shape she arrived as a gift from God. In the final six weeks of my pregnancy, I received two phone calls from friends who were out of town. Both told me the Spirit of God was prompting them to pray for me and for the baby. I never knew what was happening at that point, but we were very thankful for their prayers.

On December 5, 1984, at 1:32 p.m., Sarah Joy was born perfectly formed, beautiful, and a true miracle of God's hand. I had another cesarean section and needed to stay in the hospital a few extra days. Sarah Joy was sleeping by my bed most of the time, and all I could do was stare at her. She was so precious! I was a bit numb from the swirl of emotions I felt. On the day we took Sarah Joy home, she was wrapped up in that feminine, hand-sewn blanket I had made over a ten-year period.

In April 1985, when Sarah was four months old, the Lord awoke me one morning to tell me, "Pita is in town, staying with Laura. Get up and get your house in order; they want to come over to see Sarah Joy." God knew my house was a mess, and He knew I would be embarrassed. He sure knows His own children, and He cares even about such simple things. I got up and began to clean house. I took meat out of the freezer to fix taco salad for lunch. I waited for her phone call, and it came at about 10 a.m.

I picked up the phone and said, "Hello, Laura. I heard you and Pita are coming over today. The Holy Spirit told me." She was not surprised because she knew the ways of the Lord too. When Laura called me, I was ready, being alerted to their arrival by the Lord.

Pita was one of the prayer warriors from the Bible study group. She had prayed constantly for Sarah while she was being formed in my womb. Pita would often call and encourage me. When I answered the phone, she would exclaim, "Sister, we're going to have a baby!" I remember telling her I would ride on her faith, because mine was lacking. After all, I reasoned, I had been pregnant many times before. Pita prayed for Sarah to have pretty brown hair, since Martin had been born bald. Sarah did have brown hair. Laura and Pita arrived for lunch and our visit. Pita wanted to hold her. I watched in awe as Pita stood over the crib, worshipping the Lord as tears of joy fell from her chin and wound their way through that soft head of brown hair.

I had forgotten about my call to Contact America, but then God brought it to my attention. I decided to send them a copy of the birth announcement and a photo of Sarah Joy. I received a call and a request for a phone interview. A program on abortion was aired, and with it was the story of Sarah Joy and a mother's faith to wait on God. I still have that tape and smile when I think of the scope of God's plan.

PERSONAL REFLECTION

As I reflect on this story, I am still in awe at God's perfect love, even when we are not perfect. His unfailing, merciful love and kindness are beyond measure. The miraculous birth of our daughter was one big petal in the flower of my life God was detailing.

Our lives are not our own. And we all have an impact on others as God desires. I remember meeting a man gifted prophetically who had spoken these words to me: "I am going to change and alter the lives of many people through what I am going to do in you." I have no idea how many people this story affected because it went out through the Contact America, broadcast to hundreds of listeners along with many others who heard my testimony. Notice that it is God's work in me, not my work! He is the focus, not me.

The sweet blanket would become Sarah's security blanket that she carried around during her childhood years. It was wrapped around her dolls and even got lost one night. After prayer, we found it in the yard tucked under a bucket where she had left it while playing. Today, I have a remnant of that worn-out, colorless piece of cloth tucked in a zipper bag in the bottom drawer of a dresser. I'm kind of sentimental about that precious piece of cloth.

Sarah Joy is indeed a joy to the King of kings. She has a tender heart toward the Lord and a wisdom beyond her years. She shares her father's love of Bible prophecy and is actively involved in church ministry. She is not only my daughter, but she is one of my best friends. Sarah is employed at a local Christian preschool. I have so many opportunities to encourage couples who have fertility issues, giving them hope in trusting God. I saw the perfect timing of God in how He waited for the ladies' Bible study to come together so they would also be impacted by this answered prayer. He was once again detailing my life with this miraculous answer to prayer to give me another testimony.

"For My thoughts are not your thoughts, Nor
are your ways My ways," says the Lord.
"For as the heavens are higher than the earth, So are My ways
higher than your ways, And My thoughts than your thoughts."
—Isaiah 55:8–9 (NKJV)

Dave with Martin and Baby Sarah wrapped in the hand sewn blanket.

CHAPTER 19

HEALING CHILDHOOD SCARS

There were events in my childhood I had chosen to block in my memory, but the impact was eating away inside of me. I will not share the details here for the sake of protecting those involved. But results of the damage done to me caused a deep root of bitterness. I was a very angry woman, and when anyone pushed the right button, I would explode. Satan is a master at lying to our minds, and he had me convinced to shut my mouth and ignore my pain. So, quiet I kept, but the damage was being done deeply within my mind and soul and body. Hatred became my vent, and self-rejection was my companion. Trust was something I did not give even to my husband. Here is how the Lord healed me.

God brought my sister into my life after an eleven-year absence. In her concern, she offered to set up private counseling sessions for me. I had never been to a counselor before and did not put much trust in the whole idea. The appointment was arranged, and I waited with trepidation for the day to come. Inside I was a basket case, but how could I open up my heart to a stranger? How could I tell this man the things that were eating at me, and how would I stop myself from vomiting out every emotion that I had stuffed for so long? I could not even figure out my own issues or identify every hole inside of me so, how could they? I went to the counselor's office, and he just happened to look like one of the people who had hurt me. As he shut his office door, I shut my heart and my mouth. On the way home, all I could think of was that Jesus Christ was the best counselor of all time. He would do His work in me better than a human could.

My husband questioned me when I arrived home, and he agreed that we needed to trust God to do His work in me, and it didn't take long. The Lord was already at work on this situation. Here is how God healed me. I was given free tickets to a water park in Federal Way. I took my kids for the day, and while sitting alone at a small table watching Sarah wade in the pool, I was approached by a lady from my church. I knew who Laura was but didn't know her personally. Laura was a mature woman of God and very discerning. She had been praying for me, almost a complete stranger to her. She was given a free ticket to the park as well; the Lord had spoken to her to wait, and He would show her when to go and whom He wanted her to pray with.

Laura asked permission to sit beside me. She began to talk with me about her own testimony, and then she approached the subject head-on. God knows each of us so intimately, and He knew the kind of person to whom I would respond. He chose Laura because she understood my pain. As Laura obeyed the Holy Spirit's prompting, she gently opened up my inner pain. Laura walked me through forgiveness and repentance. I cried out to God and forgave those who had hurt me so deeply and to forgive myself for the years of bitterness and resentment. Laura opened up her Bible, and in two hours that day around that table, God did more for me in the process of healing my emotions than I could have ever experienced in any other way. I literally felt like I had shed several pounds of emotional baggage.

PERSONAL REFLECTION

Who would have thought the Prince of Peace, Jesus, would show up on a spontaneous trip to a water park where He would prune off many decayed petals in my heart? This part of the carnation was a critical area of healing for me. Since this touch of the Holy Spirit in my life, I am able to minister in compassion and understanding to many other women who have endured the same painful experiences and memories.

The Lord is so precious and filled with mercy for those who hurt. It is true that we are like an onion and God peels us open and heals us one layer at a time. No wound is too big for God to heal. The only thing needed is a willingness to let Him come into those wounded areas.

The bitter root inside me was dug up that day; God was attending to this very important detail. The peace planted in its place is a sweet aroma to Him. It's not that those old thoughts and emotions don't try to rise up at times, but I take them captive and begin to pray for those involved. Sometimes we are so impatient, giving God our timetable, instead of realizing that it is His timetable and His way. Oh, how merciful is our God, how understanding and patient.

Therefore if the Son makes you free, you shall be free indeed!
—John 8:36 (NKJV)

CHAPTER 20

A High School Crush and Emotional Soul Ties

When I was a sophomore in high school, I met a young man I developed a crush on. This young man attended a local church that was on my *good list*. We were in the same study hall seated across from each other. We had several conversations, and I was so hungry for affection I leaned on his every word. I found myself thinking about him a lot, and when summer came, I realized just how much I was looking forward to reconnecting when school started again. But as my mother told me, it is one of two ways with love. It is either *absence makes the heart grow fonder* or *out of sight out of mind*. And we were out of sight, and I was out of his mind all summer. In the three months of summer vacation, he had found another love. My heart was broken, and upon returning to school to begin my junior year, I met the other woman.

His new love, Angie, made my life miserable because a friend had betrayed my trust and told her of my feelings for her boyfriend. The remaining two years of high school were hard because I walked around all day, every day with this hurt and sense of rejection. Once again, I was not good enough; that was how I felt in my heart.

Fuel was added to my emotional vulnerability through other events too. One Saturday I was walking downtown and saw this couple coming toward me, hand in hand. As my stomach hit the ground, Angie glanced up and saw me. She turned him aside to look into the window of a jewelry store and began to talk loudly about her engagement ring as I walked by.

Then there was Valentine's Day! The youth groups of both churches decided to combine their Valentine's Day banquets. I knew they would be attending as well, and, as usual, I had no date! But I had dropped quite a bit of weight and was looking pretty good, or so people said. During the time that I had been dieting, I would exercise in my room to a song by Diana Ross, "Someday We'll Be Together." So I decided to go to the banquet and strut my stuff! Yes, they showed up and sat across the room from me. I tried not to stare at them but knew my face was red, and I definitely could feel the heat of it. I went into the ladies' room only to have Angie follow me inside. She looked into the same wall mirror I was gazing in and said, "I think you should know that we'll be married within a year." You have to understand that Angie and I were never friends, so I believed that her comments were meant to hurt me.

All of this was drama and silly girl stuff! That poor guy had no clue he was the object of so much competition. But life moved on, and I set my focus toward graduation. I still felt resentment for Angie and rejection from my crush. The hotbed of fantasy was being laid in my mind, and it would grow a good crop! I had no idea that a stronghold was forming deep in my soul. After graduation, my family moved to Alaska, where I met and married Dave. We decided to take the Alaska ferry to Seattle and drive to my hometown. I still secretly desired to move back there; the angry vow I made to live there was still working inside of me. I heard through the grapevine that my high school crush had broken up with Angie and had married someone else.

My joy and spite knew no limits as I thought of the pain Angie must be feeling. I was very smug and laughed about her misfortune and wanted a chance to rub her face in it. I really wanted to run into Angie and shine my wedding ring in her face, wishing it could happen right in front of that same jewelry store. Spite was firmly planted in my heart, and I did not consider it sin at this point. I was feeling pretty good about my handsome husband, and I wanted to show him off, especially to the one who had been so nasty to me.

I would think about this event, and feelings of resentment would surface against Angie and my former crush. Years passed, and even though I was married and had a young son, I was still burning with scorn and rejection. This area of my soul was not on the surface, but it was still alive inside. I would dream about meeting my crush again and showing him what he had missed. My imagination was out of control! I had my own high school soap opera in my mind. But the God I loved was seeing through this area of my heart too. He had a plan to remove my bitterness and add another petal to my heart bearing a sweet fragrance.

It was a Sunday morning in 1983. Dave and I were in our Sunday school class at our new church home. As I sat beside my husband, I heard a faintly familiar voice behind me. I turned around and looked into the face of my high school crush, and beside him was his wife. I could feel the red heat climbing up my neck. My heart was beating out of my chest, and I wanted to both run and stay at the same time. I remember praying and telling God I didn't like this one bit! But I knew He would never hurt me and I could trust Him through this situation too.

I spoke not a word to him that morning but went home and called a close friend to get her insight and wisdom. Deana laughed at me and told me to go right up to him next week and say, "Hello, long time no see," and allow God to do what He wanted to do. I told Deana a flat "No!" and hung up the phone. I was the heaviest I had ever been and did not want to face this man. My current reality was not matching up to my fantasy. But God softened my heart throughout the week.

The next Sunday, they were at my church once again. I chose to let God do His work in me. I walked up to him as Deana had suggested and began to talk to him. I reminded him of who I was, but he did not recognize me at all. I was shocked into reality once again. After a little small talk, he introduced me to his wife; she was so sweet. They had three children, and I could tell that he had grown into a deeply committed man of God. I saw the family across the sanctuary, and he was worshipping with all of his heart. God was doing a deep work within me that morning. It felt so sweet as I worshipped and repented all at the same time. I was getting an attitude adjustment Jesus style! Dave and I talked to this special couple several times and found that we had quite a lot in common. However, before we could invite their family over for dinner, they returned to their former town. My eyes were opened wide, and I was refreshed to see the truth up close and personal.

PERSONAL REFLECTION

The Lord pulled down the mental fantasy, showing me the truth of the matter and how blessed I was to have Dave. He brought me to repentance and showed me how important it is to guard my mind and not allow any issues of the past to become bigger than life. I chose to forgive Angie for her attitude toward me and also forgave myself. I learned the freedom of saying the words, "I have been so wrong!" I have not returned to this scene in my mind for years, and the freedom of it is sweet. The human heart can truly conceive lies that will destroy us if they are not dealt with.

As for you, my son Solomon, know the God of your father, and serve Him with a loyal heart and with a willing mind; for the Lord searches all hearts and understands all the intent of the thoughts. If you seek Him, He will be found by you; but if you forsake Him, He will cast you off forever.
—1 Chronicles 28:9 (NKJV)

CHAPTER 21

ANGELS SHOW UP ONCE AGAIN

I had been teaching our children about the angelic forces around us and about God's protection. Through an unexpected event, He made this a true-life experience. Martin, Sarah, and I had gone to K-Mart and were coming home when the front tire on our car blew out. Dave was working forty-five minutes from us, and we were stranded for a ride home. I didn't even have time to pray, and as I got out of the car, I noticed a white sedan pulling up behind me. Two men in white uniforms got out of their car and began walking around my car. They were not wearing ID badges, and their countenance was radiant. They didn't speak one word to me but were surveying the situation. One of them opened the trunk and looked for a spare tire. Finding none, he spoke to me and told me they were taking us home.

It was as if they were on an assignment and knew when we would be at that spot and were waiting for us to arrive. I was in total peace and did not argue the point. After my children and I were in the backseat, we began the trip home. The men knew where we lived and had the car radio tuned into a local Christian station. The man in the front passenger's seat began a conversation with Martin about his homeschool program. The ride home was quick and intense; I was very aware that the men knew us well. I began to sense this was just one more of God's divine appointments. There was no fear but a sweet sense of calm. We thanked our two new friends and walked into the house. We looked out the window and realized they had vanished. There was not enough time for them to back out of our driveway, get out of our yard, and down the road. There was no sign of the men in uniform, and we were very aware we just had an angelic visitation.

I turned on the local Christian radio station, and the song "Angels Watching over Me" was playing. There was a precious and sweet awareness of God's love throughout our home during the rest of the day. When Dave arrived home that evening, we had a discussion about angels and their position in God's kingdom. The following day, we both had the same encounter with the Holy Spirit at the same time, but Dave was at work, and I was at home. I felt prompted to look up Hebrews 1:14 and read that angels are spirit messengers sent by God to protect those who will come into salvation. At work, on his morning break, Dave felt prompted to turn to the same scripture. We were both excited to realize God was talking to us and had chosen to enter into our conversation about angels. He is always interested in His children.

PERSONAL REFLECTION

The Lord had been present in our living room the evening before and had entered our conversation, confirming to both of us that indeed He has given His angels charge over us. This experience would prove invaluable to me in the years to come.

Do not forget to entertain strangers, for by so doing
some have unwittingly entertained angels.
—Hebrews 13:2 (NKJV)

CHAPTER 22

DAVE'S MYSTERY GIFT

The Lord gave me an idea for a special Christmas present each year, and I began to call it the *mystery gift*. Dave and I went to the Puyallup fair together, and he was paying a lot of attention to the hat booth. He really loved Stetson hats with the colored logo of the cowboy giving his horse a drink of water out of his hat. Now in 1990, these hats cost a lot of money, and he knew that to buy one was only a dream. He made the choice to be the only one working so I could be at home with our children. As a child Dave spent many nights without either parent because they were working. He ate cold peas and soda crackers and waited for his parents to arrive home. He did not want that for his own children. So we sacrificed many of the items we wanted for the sake of our children.

I saw him gazing at the hats and decided right then he would be the one to receive the mystery gift. I did some babysitting, saving every spare penny I could, and purchased the hat he loved. I hid it when I got it home. When Dave wasn't home, I wrapped it up nicely and snuck it under our Christmas tree. I anxiously awaited the look on his face when he discovered the mystery gift this year was for him.

Now, we didn't drink beer, but we got a laugh out of some of the beer commercials. The one that said, "For all that you do, this

Bud's for you," came in handy as I wrote out the card that I put on the mystery gift. The card had a picture of an exhausted dad coming into the bathroom to take a bath only to find the tub packed full of kids' toys. I wrote on the card these words: "For all the early morning hours, and the tired feet at the end of your workday, for all that you do, this Stetson's for you!"

Dave tore into that box and was completely surprised! "How did you do it?" he asked. He wore that hat with pride even to church. I watched from afar as he proudly told many friends where he got his Stetson. It was such fun, and I am so thankful God gave me the idea because I didn't know what was coming in a short nine months.

Personal Reflection

It is so important to speak words of love to those close to you, as well as to do acts of kindness. I often think of that Christmas and the sacrifices made to buy the hat. I am very thankful for this memory.

A new commandment I give to you, that you love
one another; as I have loved you, that you also
love one another. —John 13:34 (NKJV)

CHAPTER 23

THE DARKEST VALLEY

The years had passed; Martin was now a teenage boy of thirteen, and Sarah Joy was almost six. I had been sensing an independence growing deeply within me. I was wishing I had an outside job and very much wanted to be more independent. And I was concerned about the gap that seemed to be developing between Dave and me. One night as we were watching a news program, we saw a story about the death of a man and the turmoil his family was facing. Dave was brokenhearted for this family, and it brought us into a discussion of all the "what ifs" should he die before me and leave me to raise our children alone. I listened attentively, and we talked for two hours about all the preparations he had made for our family in case of such an event.

Our mortgage company called on us, showing up at our door one evening unexpected. We made an appointment with them. During that meeting, we signed up for mortgage insurance. We did not sense any impending doom but knew it was a wise choice. If Dave or I died, our home would be paid in full. God's providence initiated this meeting and the timing of it. He sent our mortgage company to us unexpectedly,

August brought some hard times for our family, and Dave and I talked about returning to Alaska. The words to an old hymn began to play in my mind. I stopped by my church to look up the song in the hymnal and had the office worker copy it for me. The hymn was: "I Know Who Holds Tomorrow." That night, I sang it to Dave, and we took comfort in knowing we were not alone in our needs and decisions.

Friday, September 7, 1990, was a busy day. We were planning to have company the next evening, so I was cleaning, preparing food, and getting ready for their visit. We had a special time when Dave came home from work; he was rolling around on the floor playing with the kids. After tucking them in and praying over them, Dave returned to the living room to say good night. Morning comes early for a mailman. He turned to leave the room, then stopped and came back. He laid his hands on my head and prayed, "Lord, give Donna wisdom and strength." At that, Dave turned and walked down the hallway to bed.

After rising the next morning at five and telling me goodbye, Dave hugged Martin in the hallway and was out the door to work. The day passed quickly. I placed my favorite casserole in the oven and awaited his arrival home. Our company would be here in one hour.

I put a video of Alaska in the VCR and was prepared to tell Dave I would agree to return to Alaska if he wished. At approximately 4:20 p.m., there was a knock at the back door. Martin and Sarah answered it and came to get me. I saw a strange man standing in the doorway, with another man standing behind the door. The words were forever branded into my mind. The man introduced himself as a chaplain from Pierce County Police, and at that moment, Dave's supervisor stepped out from behind the door. The chaplain said, "We are sorry to tell you that your husband, David, died in his truck this morning at 7:30 a.m." I took a few steps backwards to brace myself on the washer and dryer and the chaplain continued to talk to me.

It took me a few moments to wrap my mind around the words. Dave was dead! He entered eternity instead of coming home! Martin fell into the arms of Dave's supervisor, and Sarah began asking, "Where is Daddy?" My first words were, "Oh, Jesus!" In the darkest times, the only word worth saying is Jesus. He had passed away of focal severe arteriosclerosis at the age of forty-two. The coroner said it was highly irregular for a man his age to have such an advanced stage of heart disease. It is called the silent killer for a reason; we had no idea Dave was so sick.

My husband had not even signed in at work that day. He had told his supervisor he was going home. No truer words were spoken. The chaplain told me to relax and that I didn't need to do anything right away. Because he died in another county on Federal Postal property they had taken his body to Seattle for an autopsy. But a heavenly strength permeated my being, and I began making calls to my parents, Dave's family in Alaska, and also to my pastor and personal friends. Within thirty minutes our house was filled with friends and family. The following two weeks would bring many decisions I had to make, and along with them, an inner witness as to which choice to make.

The memorial service was special beyond words and attended by approximately five hundred people. Postal employees wore their uniforms, and, along with many of our personal friends, they came to honor our family. My pastor preached from his heart, and seventeen people made a profession of faith in Jesus Christ. I stood in line to greet and thank people for approximately two hours. Steel was in my backbone as the Lord gave me the words and the strength to stand up under the pressure. Lucy, who had been Dave's supervisor, was one of those who personally greeted me, and I thanked her for hiring Dave. She was surprised I knew her, and she told me Dave was one of her favorite employees.

I could not sleep the night after Dave's memorial service. My sister and I talked until the early hours of the morning. I did not know what the future held, but I knew who held that future in His hands. The Lord reminded me of the song "I Know Who Holds Tomorrow." We sang this song at the memorial service. It became my theme song for the first few years of my widowhood.

I needed some income immediately, and I went to search for some spare change in Dave's dresser drawer. I was very shocked to see his bonus paycheck lying on the bottom of the drawer. It was signed and ready to cash. I knew from experience Dave did not just leave signed checks lying around. He was very cautious about financial matters. This was a gift from the Lord, and I knew it.

I thought about the angelic visitation the kids and I experienced just a few months earlier, and I thanked God again. I also knew that remembering God's past faithfulness to me would prove invaluable when the days got tough. And the days did get tough, especially in the grieving of my children. Martin held in his grief and did not know how to vent it. I sought out counseling for him, and to my disappointment, the counselor also died of a heart attack shortly after Martin began to open up to him.

Sarah awoke night after night, crying for her father. Finally, I decided to bring her to bed with me until she could again sleep through the night. I made a bed for Martin in my room as well. We needed to be together. I had a drive within myself to pull my children into a safe place, alone with me to recover, lick our wounds so to speak. I wanted everyone to just leave us alone so we could catch our breath. But I also wanted people to help us. I wanted to run but there was no place to run. I had to face the road ahead.

Two weeks after Dave's memorial service, I received a call from the post master in Auburn. He told me Dave had been recommended for carrier of the year. The approval of this honor came the day after he died, but they still wanted to dedicate it to him. A very impressive ceremony was planned, and my parents went with us as we were presented with a financial award and a certificate in Dave's honor. The very person—my husband—who had been afraid to work for the Federal Way Post Office was made carrier of the year.

I knew Dave was watching from his heavenly home, and God had honored his memory. I was able to meet many of those whom he had worked with and had a chance to extend God's love to them in a time of difficulty. We walked the same last steps up that private drive where Dave had walked before he died. It was a reminder to me that we are indeed only a vapor in this life.

PERSONAL REFLECTION

Having never walked this widow's pathway, I did not know where all of the potholes in the road were. I knew God's faithfulness in the past, and I prayed to Him long and hard to have the strength and wisdom for all of the decisions and difficult days ahead. God was setting out to show me I could trust His care and that I was not alone. I was constantly thankful for the many years I had already walked with God, but fear was still there to harass me. There were many words of advice from people who meant well but I could not hear them. People said I was so strong but they had no knowledge of the many tears I cried in the night. I was in a fog and that blessed numbness preserved me for several weeks as I took one step at a time into the future. Today as I reflect on this season of my life, I can truly say that the waters were deep and high, but God's hand kept us safely tucked inside, sheltered by His protective love.

When you pass through the waters, I will be with you;
And through the rivers, they shall not overflow
you. When you walk through the fire, you shall not
be burned, Nor shall the flame scorch you.
—Isaiah 43:2 (NKJV)

CHAPTER 24

STEPPING OUT

Four years before Dave's death, the Lord brought an opportunity for us to bless a young couple he knew from work. Gary worked with Dave and was very excited that his wife was finally going to have a baby. They had also experienced fertility problems, and now they were planning to welcome a baby girl in just a few months. One day at work, Gary got an emergency call; his wife had delivered alone at home, and the baby was three months early. Mom and baby were being airlifted to the hospital, and he had to leave immediately.

When Dave got home, he shared with me about the couple, and we went to prayer right away. We understood that infertility road, and our hearts were hurting for them. Although I had never met Gary or his wife, I had a very soft place within me for them. I was drawn by the Lord to keep praying day after day. Things were critical for sweet baby Carrie, and her parents sat by her little neonatal unit continually. I thought about my friends Heather and Luke and the death of young Thomas so long before. It put fuel on the fire of my prayers.

One morning I had a deep impression from the Lord. He wanted me to go shopping for a sweet little dress, complete with a bonnet and booties. He impressed on me to get a card, told me what to write and to wrap up the package and give it to the couple. I was to tell them to bring Carrie home in that outfit, that she would live and not die.

Oh, boy! What if she died? What if I was wrong? Fear was trying to destroy any idea of obedience. I tossed and turned about taking action and decided to wait it out and see if that impression got stronger or weaker. Was this my flesh speaking, or was it the Lord? It got stronger and stronger. I told Dave what I was hearing, and he did not have a problem with it at all.

I chose to step out in faith and went shopping. I picked out a sweet lacy yellow dress with a flower applique, lacy booties, and the card. I was pleased with my purchase. I felt as if I was being led by God's "shopping eyes," as I found both the items with little effort. I wrote what the Lord had spoken, "Carrie will live and not die. Bring her home in this outfit."

Dave took the package to work and gave it to Gary. He had to return to his job while his wife and child were alone day by day in the hospital. Now, this precious young couple did not know the Lord as we did, but we felt that this gift of love to them would to speak to their hearts. We made it clear to them that it was inspired by God through our prayers. It was not our idea, but His. Carrie did live, and she wore that sweet outfit home! Her parents took a picture of her on that day and sent it home with Dave. What a precious picture it was.

I still had not met the couple, and I felt my part in the story was over. But I was wrong. On September 8, 1990, it was Gary who discovered Dave's body in his truck at the Federal Way Post Office employee's parking lot. He would be the one who ran back into the building to get help. Gary was impacted by the loss of his friend Dave in ways that I still do not know. At the memorial service, I met both Gary and his wife. They came to honor Dave and to meet me. When they introduced themselves, all I could do was take both of their hands and ask about Carrie.

PERSONAL REFLECTION

Sometimes the Lord asks us to just plant a seed in the heart of others for Him. We do not see into their souls like He does. I still have no idea how all of these events impacted this couple, but I am not the Great I Am. Like Moses of long ago, I had to learn to respond in blind obedience. God uses it all. I am His daughter, and He uses me as well. I am so glad I stepped out and obeyed his leading.

> Now therefore, go, and I will be with your
> mouth and teach you what you shall say.
> —Exodus 4:12 (NKJV)

CHAPTER 25

FORGING A NEW ROAD

After Dave's death, my mom and I made a trip to the Social Security office and applied for benefits for the children and myself. The employee was a kind old man and he held and patted my hand as he asked me for the date the marriage had ended. I couldn't focus on what he had asked me and he softly rephrased the question. "Honey, when did your husband pass away?" A deep sob came from deep inside me and my Mother had to give him the answer.

Years before, I had questioned God as to the reason he had allowed us to struggle financially for four more years before Dave was hired on with the postal service. I secretly and grudgingly disagreed with God about His timing.

Now, years later as I waited for the approval of our death benefits, I learned that Dave had barely made the forty quarters for paying into the Social Security plan. Had he gotten hired on at the post office earlier than he did, I would not qualify for both the Social Security Survivors income as well as the Postal Annuity. I heard in my heart a soft answer from the Lord. "See Donna, I knew what you would need a long time ago."

Even way back then, God was planning ahead for our family. Otherwise I would only have half of the income I would need to provide for our family. Thank you Jesus, you are so wise!

PERSONAL REFLECTION

I knew the scripture about God being a husband to the widow, but what exactly did that mean anyway? This was not a fun situation, and I began to feel the pain of the reality of it. This was out of my control, and I felt like my insides were hanging out and I had a deep wound, bleeding and gaping open, that I could not heal.

> For your Maker is your husband, The LORD of hosts
> is His name; And your Redeemer is the Holy One of
> Israel; He is called the God of the whole earth.
> —Isaiah 54:5 (NKJV)

> A father of the fatherless, a defender of widows,
> Is God in His holy habitation.
> —Psalm 68:5 (NKJV)

CHAPTER 26

CHRISTMAS WITHOUT DADDY

I was dreading Christmas this year. Dave had been dead for only a few months, and we were very numb and lonely for him. The hole he left was painfully obvious. Martin had written me a note saying we needed to celebrate Christmas in a big way this year. I knew he was hurting, and to be able to look forward to something was important. I asked my friends for suggestions to make the day special and finally decided to cook a special dinner with the kids helping me. I also felt we needed to get out of the house and do something extraordinary. I made reservations at a local hotel with a pool. I promised my kids they could teach me how to swim. We were all trying to be happy, but our sorrow was ever present.

Early Christmas Eve, our doorbell rang. It was one of Dave's coworkers from the Federal Way Post Office. He brought us a special collection that was taken up by the employees. Each year they adopted a family, and this year they had chosen us. There was a gift certificate to the Tacoma Mall, various fruits and candies, and a card they had all signed for us as well. What a special thing to do! We said our thanks, and the man left the house.

Into the kitchen we went. I had purchased a very small turkey and prepared it for the oven, both kids at my side. I pretended the turkey was trying to fly away, flapping its naked wings around squealing, "Help me! Eat beef!" Both of my kids looked at me like I had lost it! They knew I was only trying to lighten up the mood. We had Christmas movies playing on the VCR and set the table for our dinner. Later, in the early evening, we ate and then piled into the car and left for the hotel. There was no hustle and bustle at the hotel, as I expected. Everyone was with family, and we were practically alone. It was cold, dark, and lonely. Bad idea!

I had purchased bubble bath for Sarah, new pajamas for everyone, and a special movie to watch after we swam in the pool. Our friend Denise had brought us a basket with treats to enjoy at the hotel. She was the children's minister at our church and wanted to bless us. We had the pool to ourselves. Isolation was not what I had in mind when I had made these plans. No, I did not learn how to swim, but both of my kids tried hard to teach me.

No matter how much we did to feel better, the sorrow was there. In the morning, we returned home and settled in for the day. Being in our familiar surroundings helped us all. I was so glad when the holidays were over and we could return to a more normal schedule with school starting again. Life just had to get better. We needed to feel better! We still did not know what "normal" would look like at home ... only God knew.

Personal Reflection

I tried so hard to hide my feelings behind activity. I painted rooms, redecorated the house, and built a carport. I kept busy doing, going, and hiding from the pain. What I really needed to do was lay down and rest and pray. It would have helped me so much more.

The Lord is my shepherd; I shall not want. He
makes me to lie down in green pastures;
He leads me beside the still waters. He restores my soul; He
leads me in paths of righteousness For His name's sake.
—Psalm 23:1–3 (NKJV)

CHAPTER 27

FRESH SORROW—RECEIVING THE COMFORT OF OTHERS

I felt so strong right after I was widowed. It was as if steel had been poured into my backbone. But after a few weeks, I began to soften, and the sorrow of loss engulfed me. At first I sat right up in the front row at church each Sunday because I wanted to soak up God's presence, but I began to feel very aware that I was alone.

My friends sat with their husbands, his arm around her, and that made me cry. Fathers picking up their little children in their arms after the service made me cry. One Sunday, Sarah saw her little friend run up to her daddy, and he picked her up. My Sarah began to sob, "My … my … my daddy!" People around her began to comfort both of us.

I began to sit further back in the sanctuary near the side door. My plan was to exit as soon as I could and escape to the car. I told the kids to come right to the car after church. I could not handle it when people would ask me, "How are you doing, Donna?" I would say, "Oh fine." But I was lying.

One Sunday, I made my escape and almost got to my car when a sweet elderly lady from church followed after me. I heard her voice calling me as she asked, "How are you doing, honey?" I told her if anybody asked me that question again, I was going to explode! Looking me in the eyes, she asked me once again, and I let her have it! "I'm feeling crushed and torn apart with deep, intense pain that doesn't go away, my kids are crying themselves to sleep at night, and I am scared to death! I am so angry right now I could spit nails, and I don't know what to do about it all."

There in the church parking lot, rain falling, Stella reached out to me. She drew me into her warm, soft arms and held me close as I wept. It felt so good to be held and to allow myself to be real in the arms of the divine love sent to me in her embrace. Stella was on assignment from the Holy Spirit to comfort me, and I let her. I felt like a volcano, Mt. Saint Donna, and I had exploded, pouring out the lava of emotion; my soul felt released. But it was not over.

A few weeks later, I was in another time of sorrow. The waves on that ocean were threatening to capsize my emotional boat. It was also a Sunday morning, and I could not face people, especially married women and kids with daddies. I decided to just drop the kids off at church and go down to Fir Lane Memorial to gaze at Dave's grave. I thought there were no more tears to cry, but I was wrong. I just sobbed, gasped for air, and sobbed some more. I began to gag and took a few deep breaths and heard the Holy Spirit say to me, "You have been invited to the single ladies' class several times now, and you have refused to go. I have appointed that class for women to support and love on each other, and you need to drive there now."

I mopped up my face and drove back to church. The class was filled with single women. Some were never married, some divorced, and some widowed. I felt like a square peg in a round hole as I sat down. The lesson was on facing your giant. Oh, brother! The teacher wanted each lady to talk about her giant. They went around the room sharing, and of course I was the last one to speak. I drew a deep breath and said, "I do not want to face this giant, and I do not want to climb this mountain." In an instant, the floodgates opened, and I gave way to a torrent of emotion.

There were so many arms around me at that moment, so much comfort and understanding. I was not alone! And they prayed for me with great compassion and love. I felt a release—like giving birth to the enormous burden I was carrying! I felt like I was at home within the safety of this precious fellowship! The class would not last very long, as the teacher moved to another city, but during the time I was there, it was pure gold!

PERSONAL REFLECTION

I learned another lesson through these events. I was not an island unto myself. I had to let others help me carry this burden. I did not know everything. And it was vital for me to be transparent to the family of God.

Blessed are those who mourn, For they shall be comforted.
—Matthew 5:4 (NKJV)

Blessed be the God and Father of our Lord Jesus Christ, the Father of mercies and God of all comfort, who comforts us in all our tribulation, that we may be able to comfort those who are in any trouble, with the comfort with which we ourselves are comforted by God.
—2 Corinthians 1:3–4 (NKJV)

CHAPTER 28

WELCOME HOME, FAITHFUL SERVANT

Weekends were so long and hard after Dave died. The kids had no school to occupy them, and our sorrow was ever present. I could not stay home on this particular Saturday morning. There was a drive inside of me to go to the Tacoma Mall with the kids. Anything around people and out of the house was on my agenda!

I'm not a shopper. I am a "go in and get out of there" kind of person! This desire to do the mall was unusual for me, and I could not shake it, so we dressed and headed to the local mall. Saturday is always a very busy day at the mall with large crowds and special events. This Saturday, there was an art show with various forms of artistic talent displayed in every available spot. We started wandering down one of the hallways and stopped abruptly. Right in front of us was a very large painting, approximately four feet by six feet. It was absolutely breathtaking! Let me describe it for you.

It was a watercolor in various shades of greens and blues, gold, and light pink. In the background, I saw planets, stars, and clouds. Coming from the earth were streams of light showing angels accompanying souls into heaven. In the midst of the clouds, I saw a man kneeling before a figure, which I knew was Jesus. He was wearing a crown and was dressed in a white robe. A powder-blue sash was draped over His shoulder and wrapped around His waist. He was leaning down, reaching out his hands as if to embrace the man and lift him to an upright position. There was a deep expression of love on the countenance of Jesus, and there was a radiant smile on the man's face. Surrounding this scene, I saw a host of angels too numerous to count. In the lower right corner of the painting were three angels sounding trumpets. Another angel stood behind the man, holding a robe and a crown, preparing to put it on him. The picture gave me the feeling that this person had just arrived in heaven.

The painting drew me in as I stood still in front of it. Once again my tears began to flow. The artist came over to us. She was a very pleasant middle-aged woman. Her countenance was so peaceful and loving. She asked my name, and I introduced myself as well as my children. Then she began to speak to me. "You are the one God told me about! I was on vacation in Hawaii and had decided yesterday to miss this art show, but God would not let me. He said He had someone for me to minister to today. You're the person He told me about, honey." She then asked me to hold her cash box and said she would be right back because she had something for me in her car. I was surprised that she would ask me to do that for her since I was a stranger; but at that moment, she was following God's direction, and He knew I was an honest person.

In a few moments, the artist returned with a twelve-by-sixteen-inch copy of this picture and gave it to me free of charge. She hugged each of us and told us that we would be just fine because God was with us. The name of the picture is *Welcome Home, Faithful Servant*. Unfortunately, I have been unable to find the artist to ask her permission to include a copy of her painting in this book.

PERSONAL REFLECTION

I remembered what Dave's co-worker told me when he found Dave in his truck the day he died. He said Dave had a big smile on his face. I can only imagine who he saw coming for him as his body lay on the front seat of his truck that morning when he went home.

I am so thankful for servants of God who listen to His prompting and choose to obey and bless people they have never met. God moved in an amazing way to bring comfort to us when we were in need. The impact of this event lingered for years. I had the picture professionally framed, and it is hanging in my office. It was a great honor for me to be given such a precious expression of the heart and love of God as He so carefully wove another detailed petal into my life.

> Precious in the sight of the Lord Is the death of His saints.
> —Psalm 116:15 (NKJV)

CHAPTER 29

GET SARAH!

I continued to keep very busy, trying to ease the pain in my heart. One day I took the kids to K-Mart to buy wallpaper supplies, and Sarah went two rows across from me, looking at toys. Suddenly I heard the Lord say, "Get Sarah!" I looked over in time to see a man reach out to grab her to drag her into the bathroom. I called her name, she turned to me, and the man ran away from the area. I could see him watching us through the shoe aisle.

The mother tiger came alive inside of me. Fear gripped me, and I went to find an employee to report him. They said he had been hanging around the area for a couple of days. The manager called the police, and then he walked us out of the store. As we drove home, I talked to both kids about the importance of staying close to me in every store. But inside I was chastising myself for allowing Sarah to move over two aisles even though I could see her clearly. Even when danger is lurking, God was watching over her and being a husband to me, a widow.

PERSONAL REFLECTION

There is a song that talks about God's eyes are even watching the sparrows, and I was seeing once again how closely guarded we were. This was a good example of how God was being a husband to me. I needed a constant reminder I was not alone. Many years later, that K-Mart was having a going-out-of-business sale, and I went in to buy summer shirts for myself. Before I left the store, I went back to the same place this event happened and had a sincere thanksgiving prayer time between Jesus and me. I have so much to be thankful for!

> For He shall give His angels charge over
> you, To keep you in all your ways.
> —Psalm 91:11 (NKJV)

CHAPTER 30

IT'S ALL UP TO ME!

Now that I was a widow with school-age children, I began to realize how much responsibility was on my shoulders. It was all up to me now. I had to fill the role of both Mom and Dad. One day while putting wet clothes into the dryer, I made a decision; I was to do it all, be it all, and keep up with everything. I was to be *superwoman*! That decision drove me to the point of exhaustion. Within a short time, I was on edge emotionally. Tears were always on the surface. I was finding it hard to sleep. One night I got up to check the locks on the doors and windows. I woke up fearful someone would intrude. My doors and windows were not very secure. On my way back down the hall to bed, I dropped suddenly and passed out on the floor. When I awoke, I cried out to God, "Oh no, please, not this way, Lord; don't let my kids find me here like this!"

The pressure I put on myself needed to be lifted. It was wiser to let myself adjust to widowhood a little at a time. I could not drive myself so hard without serious repercussions to my health and family. I needed to not take things so seriously and not be so concerned about doing everything perfectly. A family member had told me I had a lot to thankful for and to just get over my sorrow. However, I knew I was not superwoman, and my sorrow was real.

The Scent of My Testimony

PERSONAL REFLECTION

Our culture puts expectations on us to be perfect in every way and keep it up every day. I was raised by a first sergeant dad who constantly pressured me to hurry up. I lived much of my childhood holding my breath, just waiting for the hammer to drop, but in reality, I am just one person with limitations. And that's okay! I have learned to keep it simple and stay in peace as much as I can.

In my distress I cried to the Lord, And He heard me.
—Psalm 120:1 (NKJV)

CHAPTER 31

TWO CHOICES, BITTER OR BETTER

Each and every day holds several choices for all of us. In life's circumstances, we all must choose whose voice we will follow. God had set me up for several truth encounters that would lay out my life path. He did not force the issue; rather He required me to choose which voice I would follow. Not only would my choices impact my life, but they would also impact the lives of both my children.

I was feeling fear, anger, frustration, and an overwhelming hopelessness in the midst of my adjustment to single parenthood. However, feelings are fickle and can change like the weather. The serious thing is that many times we make important choices based on our fickle feelings, and I did not want to do that. Once again God had a plan to lay out before me—two choices. This is what happened to force my decision.

One of the widows from my church called, asking me to breakfast. I knew who Donna S. was, but I didn't know her personally. God prompted her to encourage me, and I definitely needed it. At breakfast, I heard some very wise words I will never forget. Donna S. said, "You have two choices, my friend, bitter or better. What is it going to be?" In all honesty, some days it felt better to allow the bitter choice to rumble around within my being, but

I knew the end result of that was destruction. Overall, I chose to become better through the pain. Before too long, the Lord gave me an example of *better* and also one of *bitter*. Here is how that came about.

I was taking a couple of gifts to my parents' house in a nearby town. When I came to the street they lived on, I saw that road crews had dug up my area to park. I chose to park down the street and walk back to their house. I parked in front of a house where the homeowners had created special parking for their own guests. Now I knew it was just good manners to ring the doorbell and ask permission to park there. An elderly lady answered the door, and she had been crying. One glance at her living room walls showed me scripture plaques, and I could see this was a Christian home. I asked her permission to park, and she said, "Of course you can." I then asked her if she was all right because I could tell she had been crying. She replied, "Oh, honey, I just buried my husband." I told her I was also a recent widow and I would pray for her. She was so kind. I reached out and squeezed her hand and walked away.

No sooner had I turned away than I clearly heard "Better" in my heart. I didn't have much time to think on it because the next example was right around the corner. I had met this lady named Florence at the house of church friends for Easter dinner. These friends lived just across the street from her; they had befriended Florence and included her in family dinners for years. I walked in front of Florence's yard just in time to see her coming out of the front door yelling at me, "Donna, you never did come see me! The least you can do is come inside now!" I did not want to give her any of my time. She was obnoxious and controlling. I relented to her demand and went inside because she wanted me to see her house. Now Florence was also a widow too but a very angry one. She began to show me her house, and I noticed she had two family rooms as well as a living room. I said, "It must be nice to have two family rooms for family gatherings." Florence replied with venom in her voice "Family? Who needs a worthless family?" Well, that didn't go well! I just wanted to make some conversation because I really did not know her. I was feeling awkward.

At that point, Florence showed me her pantry where she had at least one hundred cans of tuna, six quarts of mayo, about fifty boxes of macaroni and cheese, and enough cat food to keep the humane society supplied for a month. Before I could get out of the house, she threw me one more angry comment. "Everyone's going to take advantage of you, now that you're alone. Don't trust anyone because they will rip you off!" As the door closed behind me, I again heard a voice say, "Bitter." I knew God was close to me, and He did a very good job laying before me my choices. There was no contest; *better* was my choice.

PERSONAL REFLECTION

God drew a line in the sand of my heart that day. I did not want that bitter root that was trying to invade my being. The enemy of my soul knew how to use human emotions, and he was hoping to trap me, plant that seed of bitterness, and drive a wedge between me and the future that God had planned for me. Bitterness is not from God; it is from the kingdom of evil supernaturalism, and I did not want it!

Even though there were many days when putting on a happy face was so hard, in the end I knew that God had my back and we would be all right. Walking out of this valley was by far the hardest thing I had ever done. I could not see or feel the hope that was ahead. Everyone around me still had their lives intact, and it was as if I was invisible to them. Some of my friends became distant, as if I was contagious with a disease that they were afraid of. But Donna S. obeyed the inner prompting of the Lord and took me to breakfast and spoke God's truth to me. I am so glad that she did. We are still friends, and whenever I see her, I always go out of my way to give her a hug and say thank you. On the road of my life, I am sticking to better choices, not bitter ones!

A merry heart does good, like medicine,
But a broken spirit dries the bones.
—Proverbs 17:22 (NKJV)

CHAPTER 32

ARMS AROUND ME

One month after Dave's death, the Lord moved a Christian family next door. For the next four years, this family would be a source of encouragement and help to us. He assembled my lawn mower, talked issues out with Martin, and helped me with car problems. She was a special friend and gave me hugs through the tough times. Eventually, I met other family members of my neighbors. When I needed childcare for Sarah, all I had to do was ask. They knew we needed encouragement, and they stood by me in love and prayer. All of this family continues to be a source of joy in my life today.

Another family God also used to encourage us after Dave died was Ed and Jane. We met through our church prayer ministry. Operation Desert Storm was ending, and there were pictures of reunions between children and their dads on TV as well as on the front page of the local paper. My children were crying themselves to sleep, and I was overwhelmed with sorrow. I knew if I called Ed and Jane, they would make a beeline to my door, and I really needed a long hug and a soft shoulder right then. I called Jane, and I couldn't get the words out; all I could do was sob into the phone receiver, "Please help me, I just can't do this!" Jane replied, "We're on our way, honey." They were at our home within an hour and brought a huge dinner of giant burgers and the trimmings. Over the years, Ed and Jane were great friends, and their compassion was such a blessing to us. *Side note: at the age of five, my daughter, Sarah, loved Ed's bald head, and she lovingly referred to him as Uncle Head.*

PERSONAL REFLECTION

Ed was diagnosed with brain cancer a few years later. Sarah and I prayed with him at his bedside just before his death. I asked Ed to tell Dave when he saw him in heaven that I loved him more! Dave had always gotten the final word in, but now it was mine, and he couldn't take it back!

> Therefore comfort each other and edify one another, just as you also are doing.
> —1 Thessalonians 5:11 (NKJV)

CHAPTER 33

A HUSBAND TO THE WIDOW

My father-in-law, John, came down from Alaska to help me out around the house. John was a kind and loving man, and he adored his grandchildren. He knelt by their bedside and prayed over them for a long time on each visit. On one visit, John decided I needed yard lights on my home. He purchased huge lights and set about to install them. When John returned to Alaska, I discovered the lights were flashing on and off like a Christmas tree. I grew frustrated and turned them off at the main breaker box in my bedroom closet. It would be the following summer when the Lord brought them back to my mind.

It was a Sunday afternoon, and as I was finishing the dinner dishes, I heard an inner prompting to go turn on the yard lights. The prompting got stronger and stronger until I could no longer ignore it. When I went to the closet and opened up the breaker box, I was horrified to see burn marks and to hear electricity arching. I was not sure what to do. I thought, *Oh great, Dave's dead, my kids are hurting, and now my house is going to burn down!* I knew a man from church who was a fire chief, and I called him. Within ten minutes, Les returned my call. He *just happened* to be with a friend that afternoon who *just happened* to be an electrician who *just happened* to have his tools with him. Both men were at my home within an hour and repaired the damage.

PERSONAL REFLECTION

God was proving Himself as my husband, and I could clearly see His hand at work on my behalf. I lay down on my bed after Les and the electrician left, and I cried myself into a deep sleep. There are just those times when a woman needs to vent, and this was one of them. The loneliness for Dave was intense, and my rest came with difficulty. This was not an easy road, and I was constantly learning how to lean on Jesus daily.

> Hold me up, and I shall be safe, And I shall
> observe Your statutes continually.
> —Psalm 119:117 (NKJV)

CHAPTER 34

Two Gifts from God

About three months after I was widowed, I awoke from an afternoon nap. Suddenly I heard Dave's voice very clearly. He said, "You're doing really good, honey. I am very proud of you."

Then another time, shortly after this, I was at the grave and trying to face the reality that he was really gone. I turned around to go to my van, and I clearly heard, "I am so glad you bought a minivan, honey. That was a good decision." I actually had to turn around to look because it was Dave's voice encouraging me. He had wanted to buy a van like this one the month before his death. This type of supernatural event has never happened again.

PERSONAL REFLECTION

Now some may argue this, but I know what I heard; it was sudden, unexpected, and precious. I thank God for these gifts. I will not debate this with anyone. God knew I needed this encouragement for the road ahead of me.

> Therefore we also, since we are surrounded
> by so great a cloud of witnesses,

let us lay aside every weight, and the sin
which so easily ensnares us,
and let us run with endurance the race that is set before us,
looking unto Jesus, the author and finisher of our faith, who for
the joy that was set before Him endured the cross, despising the
shame, and has sat down at the right hand of the throne of God.
—Hebrews 12:1–2 (NKJV)

CHAPTER 35

SCRAPING UP THE PIECES OF MY FAMILY

I was happy that the home Dave and I made for our children was a peaceful one, a place where both parents dearly loved their children and each other and were not afraid to show it. Ours was the house on the block where the neighbor kids gathered to play, and I was the other mom, with cookies and popsicles. Now we were broken, and pieces of us were scattered on the floor of my heart. The devastation I felt within would not go away. Home had been a place to have other families come over after Sunday church. Now there was no husband here, and I felt as if I couldn't invite *whole* families over. Who would the men fellowship with? I felt so incomplete, and Sundays were very lonely.

I decided we should make new traditions! We began to go to lunch at a local pizza restaurant after church every Sunday. We didn't want to go alone, so we invited others at church to join us. Surely we would have at least a few people who would come to enjoy fellowship. And we did! We filled up the restaurant, and the kids played games, ate, and loved the new tradition. This gave my children more influence by godly family men, and they were able to get some free hugs from the fathers of their friends.

I kept the kids busy with many activities and tried to keep things the same for them as much as I could. As the months passed, the enormity of our loss became obvious. I was homeschooling but decided to place both of my children in Christian school, and that left me home alone all day. After wallpapering the family room, painting my bedroom, and taking care of several repair jobs, I found myself with so much time to fill.

I would take out the video of the memorial service and watch it to make myself face the truth. I would go to the gravesite and look at the name on Dave's marker and cry until my insides were aching. I had thoughts that this was not real, that he was in the eyewitness protection program and would come home soon. I had to fight for reality.

On Dave's forty-third birthday, I took our children to the cemetery to honor their father. We had picked up some balloons and flowers to leave at the grave. Sarah sang "Happy Birthday" to her daddy and released the balloons. Almost instantly the balloons became entwined within a tall tree not far away. With tears in her eyes, she begged me to do something! I looked up to the sky and said with exasperation, "Really, God, haven't we been through enough already?" Without a breeze in the air, the strings unwound, and the balloons began to ascend to the heavens. Sarah began laughing, jumping up and down, clapping her hands. No person will ever be able to convince me that angels did not unwind those balloon strings.

Sarah remembered her Daddy loved coffee. We had stopped at the local grocery store before going to his grave. There on the floor she picked up a couple of coffee beans and put them in her pocket. She asked me to not follow her as she walked behind the wall where his remains were inurned. She stuck the beans into a crack in the wall and I heard her say, "Have fun in heaven Daddy".

PERSONAL REFLECTION

I had read that sorrow was like the waves on the ocean. Some days they were higher than other days. Just take them as they come, and one day it will be over. Every disappointment seemed to be a major mountain for me to climb.

The one flesh that Dave and I had become was ripped in half, and my whole being was in shreds. The pain felt like I wanted to get a pillow and hold it to my stomach to help me keep from falling apart and to feel whole again. Nothing would stop the pain but crying out to God. I drove the kids to school each morning and would cry out on the way home, "God, don't let me go, even if I am so angry with you right now. Please don't let me go because then I would be in really big trouble."

I would waver between anger and fear daily. God knew my heart, and I could count on that! We had been down so many roads together, and He knew my emotions were shattered but my spirit still loved Him. I began healing a little at a time, and I believe God was hovering over that process too. And another petal of the carnation was being woven into my testimony. This one was painful!

The eternal God is your refuge, And underneath are
the everlasting arms; He will thrust out the enemy
from before you, And will say, "Destroy!"
—Deuteronomy 33:27 (NKJV)

Fir Lane Memorial Park with Donna, Martin, Sarah

CHAPTER 36

PLEASE TELL DAVE I'M SORRY, LORD!

As time passed, I started to appreciate what a huge part Dave played in our home. Yes, he didn't put his laundry in the right place, and he snored! But the spiritual role and leadership this man had in the family was now so very empty. I began to realize how much of a pain I had been to him. I wished so many times I had paid more attention to him, let him know how much he meant to us, and to me in particular. The void in the lives of my children was painfully obvious. No matter what I did, I could never fill it.

So I went once again to the grave. As I stood there looking at his name, I prayed, "Lord, please call Dave into the throne room and tell him that I am so very sorry." Now I do not have a theological foot to stand on here, but a weight lifted off of my heart at that moment. There are some things that are just held intimately between you and God, period! It had taken five years for me to grieve out the loss of my sweet husband. He was one of a kind, precious, longsuffering, and a hardworking man of God! The empty hole was filling in, and I felt hope and strength again. I was never alone, and I knew who was going before me.

Personal Reflection

The only one who can see inside of us is God. He knows what we need to do to capture our peace, and He knows how to lead us into that place. I am so thankful I am His daughter.

"Peace I leave with you, My peace I give to you;
not as the world gives do I give to you.
Let not your heart be troubled, neither let it be afraid."
—John 14:27 (NKJV)

CHAPTER 37

BACK TO SCHOOL

When I graduated from high school in 1971, I received a scholarship to a beauty school. I enjoyed styling hair and the time spent with people. I knew I had the talent for the hands-on work, but I had a mental block for the academics. (See story "I Sure Wish I Knew God Like That.") During my short time at the beauty school, I received a lot of encouragement from a student named Justine; she was a Christian and about fifteen years older than I was. The students in the school respected her, and she became a mom to everyone, but all this ended when my family moved to Alaska.

For years, I had been tormented by feelings of condemnation because I did not finish beauty school. I felt like a failure, and my heart was heavy when I thought about it. I wanted more of an identity then just *mom* to my children or *honey* to my husband. I had several friends who were nurses, teachers, and secretaries. I had nothing to offer to the conversations during our visits. Self-condemnation was a constant companion.

Three years after Dave passed away, I was thinking about the direction I should take for extra income. I prayed and waited for the Lord to answer me. Within three weeks, the Lord arranged for me to run into an old friend who casually mentioned beauty school. Something went off in my spirit, and I became very excited. The

Lord told me to return to school and He would be with me. He also told me that I would be the Justine in this school, and He was going to give me favor. That is exactly what He did! Within two months, the younger students were calling me Momma Donna.

I was amazed at how easy it was to study, and I began to keep a running list of my grades. It was so different this time. I realized God's calling and gifts He puts in each of us holds true for His timing to fulfill them. I was getting almost 100 percent on the same academics I failed years earlier. To be with my kids, I took Saturdays off school. So after eighteen long months, I graduated with gusto. I passed the Washington State Boards with no trouble. Not only was I able to finish this time what I started back in high school, but I was able to witness for Jesus Christ and see the Lord honor my life in front of the students, both young and old.

PERSONAL REFLECTION

God restored what Satan had stolen from me. I was indeed a new person, and God had proven that to me in a big way. Five years after graduation, I was at the mall with a friend and was approached by a young woman who was a student at the school when I was there. She told me she became a Christian because of my witness; she introduced me to her husband and thanked me for being a witness of Jesus's love when we were in school. That meant more to me than the diploma I received.

> "So I will restore to you the years that the swarming locust
> has eaten, The crawling locust, The consuming locust, And
> the chewing locust, My great army which I sent among
> you. You shall eat in plenty and be satisfied, And praise the
> name of the Lord your God, Who has dealt wondrously
> with you; And My people shall never be put to shame."
> —Joel 2:25–26 (NKJV)

CHAPTER 38

FLOWERS FROM JESUS

Women can be strange creatures; many of them love to compete and brag. Valentine's week came, and the women at the beauty school were actually sending themselves flowers to compete with other students. It was crazy to watch their behavior toward one another, and I was not about to join them. However, my reality was that my sweetheart was dead and there would be no flowers for me this year. So, Monday through Thursday, I found myself grieving and crying in the bathroom at school. I kept praying that I would survive the week. Nobody knew my feelings or thoughts, nobody but Jesus!

Friday was the big day, the fourteenth. At about 10:00 a.m. as I put my client under the hairdryer, I heard someone call my name. I turned around to see a couple from my church standing by the reception desk with a large arrangement of flowers for me. I was shocked! They told me the Holy Spirit had been telling them to buy these particular flowers for me and to deliver them to my school today. We hardly knew each other. Mike and Laura simply said, "We hope this makes things easier to bear for you today." It just happened that these were the same flowers Dave always gave me, and they had no possible way of knowing that. They were red roses with tiny pink carnations, baby's breath, and green ferns. This arrangement was huge and lovely.

PERSONAL REFLECTION

The reaction of the other women at the school was wild, and I heard, "Oh, Momma Donna has a man in her life!" I told them, "Why yes I do; I will tell you all about him at lunch." I had an audience that day as I told them God had sent me flowers because I was crying in the bathroom and grieving all week. Now that was a story they will never forget, and neither will I.

For His anger is but for a moment, His favor is for life; Weeping may endure for a night, But joy comes in the morning.
—Psalm 30:5 (NKJV)

CHAPTER 39

A SIXTEEN-YEAR-OLD, A TRUCK, AND A HUNTING TRIP

When I was in beauty school, everything on the home front still needed my attention. My son began to attend public high school where he made friends with one of the school's security officers. He would come home and tell me all about Mr. Page and how he was also a youth worker at his church. I had not met this man but was so thankful for his impact on my son, who was missing his father so much. I enrolled Martin in Drivers' Education; he completed the course and was now ready to find a truck of his own.

At this time, Martin also made an agreement with a neighbor man to take the hunters course offered for minors, and he promised he would take Martin along with his son on the next deer hunt. Martin completed the course with the neighbor's son, and when the card arrived saying he had passed, he happily took it to show the neighbor. Much to his dismay, he learned that they had left for the very hunting trip they had invited him to go on and did not keep their promise to include him. We do not know why this happened, but I was one furious momma!

I told my son to get the Bible and look up every verse on the word "fatherless." He brought the verses to me. We placed our hands on the Bible, and we began to pray over them. We declared that God was now Martin's Father and asked Him for: (1) a truck and (2) a hunting trip. Amen! Then the wait began; I kept praying daily, reminding God what I had asked for and that His reputation with my son was on the line. He had many disappointments with Christian men, and I didn't want him to be disappointed with God. That may seem a little harsh to some people, but I was serious, and God knew the intent of my heart.

Also, during this time in beauty school, I was feeling very overwhelmed with studies in electricity, light therapy, skin diseases and disorders. Preparing me for state board exams, my instructors were questioning me about my knowledge several times daily. "Donna, define Paronychia. Donna, define onychomycosis (nail fungus)." I said silently in my mind, *If one more person asks me to define anything, I will explode!* In the midst of all this, I was holding on to God, who knew my thoughts and heard my prayers. I continued to earnestly pray for a truck and hunting trip for Martin.

One Sunday after church, I took the newspaper and called Martin into the family room. We circled all of the trucks within his price range, and I wrote down several questions for him to ask the seller of each truck. He made the calls himself. Truck #1 was sold. Truck #2, nobody answered the phone. Then he called about truck #3, the final one on his list. As Martin began to ask his questions, this is what I heard, "Yes, I do go to Bethel High School, and I do know Mr. Page. What? No way, this is Mr. Page? Is that the white truck with the red racing stripe you drive to work and you're selling it? Yes, I would like to test-drive it!"

As a mom of a sixteen-year-old son, I was not thrilled about a red racing stripe. Mr. Page came to our home, and I finally got to meet this special man who had taken my son under his care to encourage him. We bought the truck, and as we signed the title, Mr. Page looked at Martin and asked, "Would you like to go hunting with me and a few friends, Martin?" To say we were amazed is an understatement!

The hunting trip was so much fun for my son. He experienced real down-to-earth men of God just being themselves. Meanwhile, I was cleaning out the freezer in the garage because I had asked God to let that trip be fruitful for my son. When they returned, it was clear they did not see any deer, not even one. In my frustration, I said, "But, God, I asked You to make the trip fruitful!" I heard loud and clear: "Define fruitful to me, Donna." Once again my anxious thoughts were silenced by the wisdom of God.

Over the next week, I would listen to my son tell me how much fun he had with Mr. Page and how happy he was for his experience and for the new truck. The hunting trip was fruitful indeed, and it had nothing to do with deer meat in my freezer.

Later that week Martin went out in his new truck with his buddy. Jokingly I shouted to them that I had placed two big angels in the backseat. They both yelled back at me, "Tell them to hang on, Mom!"

Personal Reflection

We never realize when God is setting up situations and events to help us or others. He is, after all, the creator of the universe! I was in such a fog at times with all my responsibilities that I was forgetting God had me covered 100 percent every day.

A father of the fatherless, a defender of widows,
Is God in His holy habitation.
—Psalm 68:5 (NKJV)

CHAPTER 40

THE UN-GRADUATION GIFT

Martin had a tough senior year in high school. He did not get to graduate because he was two credits short. The morning after graduation, when he would have walked the aisle with his classmates, I made a trip to Dave's grave. I stood there crying and saying, "If Dave was alive, then Martin would be doing so much better and my heart would not be in pieces."

Out of the corner of my eye, I saw balloons waving in the wind where a young man named Mike had been buried. The balloons were meant to say "Happy graduation" to that young man who had died too young. The Holy Spirit spoke to my heart these words, "Donna, Mike's mother will never hug him again, but your son will be okay. Now, go to Costco and get him a tent so he can go camping with his friends."

I wiped those tears, blew my nose, and went to Costco. I presented the gift to Martin, who just stared at it in awe as I related the story to him. The tent became known as his "un-graduation gift." Our [1]God sees us, and He cares.

---

[1] God is everywhere, in everything, and with everything. This means He is omnipresent. "Where could I go from Your Spirit? Or where could I flee from Your presence?" (Psalm 139:7 AMP). "And not a creature exists that is concealed from His sight, but all things are open and exposed, naked and defenseless to the eyes of Him with Whom we have to do" (Hebrews 4:13 AMP).

PERSONAL REFLECTION

It felt like I had failed as a mother. Everything seemed so out of control. We had been a whole family, and now it all seemed to be destroyed. Oh, how wrong I was. Little by little, my emotions were healing, and deep inside me, there was a work being done by God.

O Death, where is your sting? O Hades, where is your victory?
—1 Corinthians 15:55 (NKJV)

But thanks be to God, who gives us the victory
through our Lord Jesus Christ.
—1 Corinthians 15:57 (NKJV)

CHAPTER 41

THE THRONE ROOM

As my son grew up, he made some tough choices; many of them came out of the pain of his dad's premature death. He was of age now, and I had to relinquish my desire to manage his decisions. One night, I sat on the edge of my bed crying out to God for my family. I don't know how long it lasted, but I was suddenly aware that my spirit was in the throne room of God. I could hear the words of my prayer arriving around me in the throne room at the same time I was speaking them from my bed. I knew then I was not just speaking into the air, but God was hearing and receiving my prayers. I felt comforted by that experience.

PERSONAL REFLECTION

God knows what we need, and when we need to receive it! Although this experience was very brief, it still impacts me today. God's love for me as a widow was far-reaching, and even though I grew angry at times, He never left me alone.

I know a man in Christ who fourteen years ago—
whether in the body I do not know, or
whether out of the body I do not know, God knows—
such a one was caught up to the third heaven.
—2 Corinthians 12:2 (NKJV)

CHAPTER 42

THE INSIDE SCOOP

I have asked the Lord many times to give me the inside scoop of what He is doing in the lives of my children. This is a story of one of those occasions.

While my son, Martin, was struggling to grow up, he decided to move to the state of Georgia. He had a friend there, and he thought it would be a good place for a fresh start. At the age of twenty, with two hundred fifty dollars to his name, he boarded a Greyhound bus and headed to the Peach State. Now it did not matter to me that he was of age, being twenty. To this mom, he was still that little blond-haired sweetheart of years gone by. Every mom knows just how stretchy that umbilical cord can be. Even though it's cut, in our motherliness it's still firmly connected. I began to pray about this great adventure of my firstborn.

I heard nothing from him for the first few weeks. Then finally he called me to let me know things did not work out. He was returning home. He told me he did not want me to make any comments or give my opinion about his trip. The Lord directed me not to send him money for any reason because He wanted to show my son a few things. Three days later, he arrived, and true to my word, I kept quiet. But I really wanted to know all about it—how he was and why he returned. Inquiring minds—*mine*—needed information because, after all, I had given him birth! I was about to see another example of how closely God watches everything about us. Although I trusted God, I thought He needed my help. It was several months before God showed me the inside scoop.

I was driving Martin to a medical appointment for a checkup. While he was stuffed into my Toyota's front seat, he began to talk. He said, "Well, Mom, I wasn't going to tell you about this, but God put a street preacher from Seattle beside me on the bus coming home from Georgia. He kept talking to me about Jesus, and he even bought me food! He told me that he knew I was raised by godly parents and there was a calling for ministry on my life. I could not get away from this preacher for three days!"

"Touché, Jesus!"

I was beside myself as I drove, wanting to scream, "Yay, God!" and to cry as well. But I had to remain calm and collected. I am a person who has plenty of expression, so my left arm, being out of his sight up against the door, was actively pounding my left thigh with a jubilant fist of victory. I saw God in action on behalf of Martin. His heavenly Father had everything under control, and I could trust Him with my son. Although his earthly dad was in heaven and Martin was still grieving, there was no place too far, even Georgia, where God would not watch over him.

PERSONAL REFLECTION

Martin wishes he knew the name of that street preacher who cared for him on the bus ride home. I would love to meet him and thank him as well. God knows where he is, and I am sure He has blessed that man for his love toward my son. My simple prayer for my kids is still, "Get 'em, Jesus!" God understands my heart. Martin enjoyed several jobs as he was finding his sweet spot in the world of business. Today he is married, and I am enjoying a very special friendship with him and his wife. Because of God's faithful love, we survived many rocky roads.

A man's steps are of the Lord; How then can
a man understand his own way?
—Proverbs 20:24 (NKJV)

CHAPTER 43

OUR NEW HOME

I was feeling a desire for new surroundings and a new beginning. Our mobile home was in great need of repair. I wanted to get out of it and into a regular house. I went looking all over the city, never finding what *felt* like home. On a Sunday afternoon, as my daughter, Sarah, and I were taking a drive, we saw an Open House sign. We stopped in front of a large two-story home. It was lovely, but I felt it was way beyond anything we could afford. Just for kicks, we went inside to look. The Lord's hand was on us that day, and the real estate agent showed us around. She asked me many questions, and I wondered why she was so persistent. Unknown to the agent, she was being directed by the Holy Spirit to be the wind at my back, pressing me forward. I qualified for the new house, and within two weeks of listing my mobile home, it sold.

I was finishing up beauty school at the time and I carried a picture of our new home in my pocket. It gave me hope for a fresh start and a future away from all of the memories of the old house. Every detail went fast, and in December 1994, we moved into our new home.

PERSONAL REFLECTION

In the years to come, we would meet special people here, and the Lord would use us to minister to them. They would then be used by Him to impact the lives of countless others. We prayed for a new friend for Sarah, and God answered our prayer in a simple way. She met her new best friend on the school bus shortly after we prayed. This family would be such a blessing to us, and we, in turn, would bless them in many ways. Theresa, a single mother also, became a follower of Jesus. She learned how to trust Him for her provisions and eventually accepted a position as secretary to the director of a local women's home nearby. We prayed together for so many things and watched God pursue her heart in trusting Him as her Lord. God gave Theresa a vision of a green minivan, and we looked for it until we found it, just the price the Lord showed her! Those were such fun and fulfilling years as two single mothers supported each other in God's love. They were hard years as well because we were opposed by the unseen kingdom of evil supernaturalism. We were about to learn many lessons as the Lord walked us through valley after valley.

The steps of a good man are ordered by the
Lord, And He delights in his way.
—Psalm 37:23 (NKJV)

CHAPTER 44

A NEW CHURCH AND
A NEW SEASON

Shortly after moving into our new home, I decided to change churches. I wanted further growth for Sarah and me. I chose to leave the denomination I had been raised in and prayed that the Lord would lead me to the right place. Unfortunately there had been great turmoil in the former church, and at this point in my life, I needed a more stable environment. I longed for a place of peace with more than fluff and games. I was determined to be very careful about where I would attend. I knew my Bible, and I would not be deceived by false doctrine.

Several people I knew were not happy when I left their denomination. But the Holy Spirit was directing me in this decision, and I needed to follow His voice. I had learned how to be confident in His leading, and I knew He had never misled me in the past. Friends called and invited me to Clover Creek Bible Fellowship just down the street. They encouraged me to attend for a month before making any decision. I actually stood outside of the Sarah's classroom so I could hear what was being taught. The teachers were teaching God's Word to the kids, not just entertaining them. They had order in the classroom, and I loved it. Most of all, Sarah loved it too!

Clover Creek was a Bible-teaching church, and their mission statement and beliefs were exactly like mine. I did not know how spiritually hungry I was until I had been there for a full month. It was like a Bible college and set up to train and equip members for ministry. I met many wonderful believers and was very happy to become a member. I signed up for the many classes that were being offered. One class after another was so helpful to me. I enjoyed listening to the testimonies of the people, and I felt like I had found a goldmine at my new church home.

The leadership helped me through a very serious season of spiritual growth as God began to work out His will in the church. Events transpired that would reveal to the leadership and also to me what we were really battling against in the heavenly realms. God began to teach us, and we decided to learn about spiritual warfare.

PERSONAL REFLECTION

Oh, how I loved this new church! It filled a hole in my spirit and soul I did not know was there. I was being fed the Word of God and quickly growing. It was as if a puzzle were being put together within my heart, gaining understanding of biblical concepts one at a time. Every single time, after each service, week by week, I was full of excitement with what I was learning. My daughter was also being nurtured, and that meant the world to me. I told friends that I felt like I'd eaten a spiritual Thanksgiving dinner every week. Others followed me to Clover Creek and said they did not realize how spiritually hungry they had become. Being sent by God to this church was a divine appointment.

A man's heart plans his way, But the Lord directs his steps.
—Proverbs 16:9 (NKJV)

CHAPTER 45

OPENED EYES

I had believed other people thought the same way I did. I assumed they saw issues through the same lens I did, and it bothered me if they *just didn't get it* the same way I did! I presumed they were not listening to me or even mocking me at times. I had a block in my understanding, not grasping the truth that people can see issues differently from the way I do. God saw this about me, and He began to remove it and teach me His way with the following situation.

One day in the salon while I was watching a tense moment between customers, the Holy Spirit showed me that we all see through a different lens. My world, my understanding of how to do things, think through things, and handle things is very different from everyone else's. People talk and reason out of their own life experiences. We may end up with the same conclusions, but our thought processes to get there can be different. Everyone's opinion is valid and should be heard without offense.

When God revealed this to me, it completely changed the way I understood and related to people. The first part was to shut my mouth and just really listen by giving them my undivided attention. God showed me how to be patient and follow His guiding voice, especially as people were pouring out their hearts to me. I would need this skill as time passed because I often found myself mentoring and counseling women. God requires me to speak truth and love to others, because this is what sets them free. It is a waste of time to run around in circles in order to not offend. Fear of offense is a poison that keeps people in destructive attitudes. Truth and light is who Jesus is and also who we must be. There is a way to speak to others with God's love and a genuine concern flowing from us. People can tell the difference.

Suddenly invitations to speak at ladies' events and men's prayer breakfasts began to come my way. God opened up many avenues for me to share my testimony. I believe He was testing me during this time to see if I gave Him the glory or if I would only promote myself. His glory was evident in the fruit of His miraculous detailing in my life, repairing the broken places and creating a new, sweet fragrance—the carnation called Donna!

PERSONAL REFLECTION

Did it ever occur to you that our lives are open and laid bare before God? That nothing about us ever *just occurs to God* where we are concerned. He does not forget us or take His eyes off of us. He is always working out His master plan within His redeemed ones who allow Him to do so. I love how the inner workings of the Holy Spirit turn things around inside my soul. I feel like a Rubik's cube at times as He sovereignly and gently turns my attitudes and opinions around to be conformed to His will.

Now then, we are ambassadors for Christ, as
though God were pleading through us:
we implore you on Christ's behalf, be [2]reconciled to God.
—2 Corinthians 5:20 (NKJV)

---

[2] Reconciled: to restore friendly relations, to make compatible, to be in harmony with God.

CHAPTER 46

PERSONAL TOUCH HAIR SALON

In the summer of 1995, the Lord directed me to convert half of my garage into a full-service hair salon. I was employed at a local salon, and the hours and environment were not working out for me. My children needed me at home. I did not know anything about construction, permitting, and the other details required for an in-home salon business. I surveyed the garage downstairs and went to the county annex building to get the direction and permits I needed to build the salon. I took a number and sat down to wait my turn.

I felt way out of place, I was a widowed hairstylist surrounded by professional contractors. I didn't even know what to ask for. I didn't know the proper terms to use either. So I prayed for Gods help. They finally called my number, and I walked up to the window to see a man wearing a T-shirt that said, *Jesus Christ, Mighty Counselor*. I began to cry as I spouted out, "I really like your shirt!" This kind man graciously led me through the details of the permitting process. I applied for bids from a few contractors, but the Lord had someone special in mind. A man at my church would be used of the Lord to do the work. This wonderful man told me he was going to do it free of charge! I was so blessed by his generosity. My father-in-law called from Alaska and gave me an early inheritance without my asking, and it financed the building of Personal Touch Hair Salon.

During the construction of the salon, a leak developed in my roof. I had no idea how to fix it but set out to find where the hole was. Up into the crawl space I went. I found the spot ... three nail holes caused by the removal of an antenna. The top of my roof was black, and I had to see the holes to fix them. I had a great idea and took three Q-tips into the crawl space and shoved them up into the holes so I could spot them on the black rooftop. Hey, whatever it takes to get the job done! My next move was to go the hardware store and buy some tar type stuff and one of those spreader things ... I was learning on the job and didn't know the right terms. The sales lady called it mastic and said I needed a trowel. I thought she said *trial*; I told her, "Yes it was a trial for sure." She just rolled her eyes at me. I had what I needed to make the repair, and the task was completed successfully.

Shortly after the start of the remodeling project, I began to sense a dark, menacing spirit around me. I could feel that something was wrong, but I didn't know what it was. I heard from a friend that the homeowners near me did not want a business coming into the neighborhood. Even though it was legal, the anger that rose up in the neighborhood was more than I expected. A few of the homeowners who were unhappy just happened to have permitting violations of their own. They were afraid of the city inspectors coming around to view my progress. But I knew I was to mind my own affairs and proceed with the construction. The suspicion died down, and the neighbors busied themselves with other things. Finally, the salon was finished, and clients were making appointments. I was so excited for this new milestone in my life and was looking forward to the people the Lord would send me for His personal touch.

I put up a business sign on the street corner, and during the night, someone destroyed it. After replacing the sign with plenty of rebar and cement, I thought that would be the end of the problem. I put my focus on taking care of my home and business. Within four weeks, a small truck had hit my sign and smashed it to pieces. Once again, I bought a new sign and put it up, only to have it vandalized shortly after. At that point, I clearly sensed the Lord telling me that He would send the customers I needed and not to put another sign in that old location. I only put a small sign in my front yard to identify the correct house for my new customers.

I had met a particular neighbor who kept coming to the salon and calling me several times daily. My heart went out to her because she had gone through a lot of religious negativity and abuse growing up. She did not understand who Jesus really was, and this broke my heart. I will not share all that transpired but only to say that I learned how important it is to stand in the truth of this verse:

> Finally, my brethren, be strong in the Lord and in the power of His might. Put on the whole armor of God, that you may be able to stand against the wiles of the devil. For we do not wrestle against flesh and blood, but against principalities, against powers, against the rulers of the darkness of this age, against spiritual hosts of wickedness in the heavenly places. Therefore take up the whole armor of God, that you may be able to withstand in the evil day, and having done all, to stand. (Ephesians 6:10–13 NKJV)

I was now busy building my customer base, taking classes at my church, and doing a personal study on understanding my authority as a believer in Jesus Christ. I held fast in knowing I was protected from all the onslaught of retaliation that was coming at me from neighbors. I was witnessing the truth about Jesus Christ to one particular neighbor. This was stirring up anger in the unseen world of evil supernaturalism. I wanted to understand what was going on and to stay in the peace that surrounded me. I knew I was in a war of a supernatural dimension; I could feel it.

Early one morning at approximately 1 a.m., an event in my bedroom would confirm how closely the Lord was guarding me. I woke up feeling a dark and hateful presence in my room. I could hardly breathe. I slowly reached up and turned on my stereo to worship music, and suddenly I saw several pairs of bright silver, gold, and diamond-edged swords cross over my face. I knew that I was not alone and did not have to fight this attack by myself. I fell into a deep sleep and woke with peace the next morning. Now, I had heard of such experiences before but never thought I would have one. The following day, I talked to the one of the leaders of my church, and he brought a team of people over to pray through my home.

The Lord prompted me to get out of bed earlier than usual and to spend more time in prayer and reading my Bible. I put on a video called "In His Presence" by Moody Press. The scenery and music calmed my soul as I read my Bible and prayed. I began to crave more times like these. God was filling up my spiritual gas tank for the years ahead. He knew I needed more time with Him.

This was just one sign of things that were changing for me spiritually, along with the healing and deliverance ministry happening at my church. We had a choice to either let Jesus teach and train us to stand in His power and authority against the powers of darkness in victory or shelter ourselves in church activity as the norm. Along with my church leadership and other members, I said yes to God's calling to fully live in the principles of His kingdom. A tremendous season of growth and change came to my church. Some were afraid of the change and left, but I stayed because I knew this was of God, and I wanted every bit of it. I was tired of my past experiences with organized church programs without power.

I wanted to live the book of Acts today! I knew that Jesus came for people, not programs or buildings.

People began bringing their family members to church for special prayer, and they were set free from oppression one by one. We had big conferences where hundreds came from all over the world, supernaturally led there by God. The revival[3] that came during this time was far above anything I had ever longed for or thought I would experience. My heart and soul have not been the same since. Out of that move of God, three churches were birthed and many lives radically changed. Several ministry books were written by the leadership, and an international ministry was birthed by the Lord.

A time came when my entire church family relocated several miles away from my area because they needed to follow the Lord's leading. I was not able to make the move with them. I felt that I was to stay behind and be with my parents through Dad's death. I cannot tell you the depth of pain I felt when my church family was gone. They were following God's call, and it was difficult to stay behind. I could not see what lay ahead for me, but past experiences told me God has a plan and purpose for everything.

All of this took place while I was taking care of the family needs in my home and working in my salon. People would come in for a haircut and comment about the peace of God they sensed. They would send in friends to "just feel" the presence of Jesus. It all meant so much to me! I wanted more of God's presence and leading. I could not go backward. I had to go forward as the Lord led me.

---

[3] Revival is understood in many different ways. For me, it means to rekindle the fire of God that has become dormant within our hearts. It is a visitation of the Holy Spirit penetrating our spirit, bringing renewed love and passion for God as our first love. It refreshes our spirit with revived energy for the things of God and His Word.

PERSONAL REFLECTION

Through the years that I owned Personal Touch Hair Salon, it seemed as if I was on the fast track of spiritual growth and ministry from the start of construction to the day I moved in and throughout all the seasons I was in business. I am so glad I experienced every event that happened; I received a personal touch from Jesus through each person who came, as well as having many opportunities to minister His love to them. I will share more of these blessings with you in the following story.

And He said to them, "Go into all the world
and preach the gospel to every creature.
He who believes and is baptized will be saved; but
he who does not believe will be condemned."
—Mark 16:15–16 (NKJV)

CHAPTER 47

LESSONS IN COMPASSION AND OBEDIENCE

The Lord was faithful to His promise to bring me customers for the twenty-one years I continued working in Personal Touch Hair Salon. Each person that came was there by a divine appointment on God's calendar, not just mine. One lady who came in revealed to me that she had heard a voice tell her to get her hair cut at my salon. She began to cry, telling me she had just buried her husband and she was sure I would not understand. Not only did she get her hair done, but I was honored to pour God's love into her heart as I gave her my own testimony of being a widow.

As business goes, there are slow weeks when the income is not there. One week I had only twenty dollars in the cash box. I received a call from a lady who lived down the street. She told me she had a heart problem and was waiting for a heart transplant. She said she had not been able to wash her own hair for several months and was desperate to have it done. Other salons would not touch her hair for fear of lice. She asked me to meet her outside my shop and examine her head. If she didn't have lice, then would I please shampoo her hair? I knew I was to agree to help her out. She didn't have lice, so I shampooed her hair five times. I also felt impressed to give her a free haircut. All during her appointment, I told her of God's love. She cried and said she had given up on God. I told her God would never give up on her, and she allowed me to pray with her. She received Jesus as her Lord that day in my salon. After I finished her hair, the Holy Spirit made it clear to me that I was not to charge her at all, and I was to also give her the single twenty-dollar bill in my cash drawer. I told her to get a Bible with the money she brought to pay me plus the extra twenty dollars. She hugged me and cried. Her husband went with her to get a new Bible.

My phone began to ring after she left, and I booked several perms that afternoon. God was taking good care of me once again. There were so many divine appointments in Personal Touch Hair Salon. Customers began to send their family and friends just to sense the presence of God. I had dedicated my salon to the God's glory when I opened in 1994. It was really never about hair; it was all about the people whom God loved and sent to my salon for His personal touch.

One older woman came each Friday at 10:00 a.m. for a shampoo and set. I will call her Jenny. Her husband, Hugh, brought her in, and he would sit and talk to me as I did her hair. They told me stories of their life raising kids in a nearby town and how they missed the good old days. After one appointment, Jenny asked me if she could borrow the Bible I had on the desk. She returned it a month later. She had given her heart to Jesus and was baptized in her childhood church. I was thrilled! Hugh thought that was nice for her but not for him.

One Friday, not long after this, I was preparing for Jenny and Hugh to arrive when I heard some commotion at the end of my street. I went out to see a fire truck and a couple of aid cars arriving. I needed to see if I could help Jenny and Hugh find another route to my salon. A city bus had rear-ended a white car, and it was smashed and laying in the ditch. I recognized the car as belonging to Jenny and Hugh. The smell of gasoline was strong; aid personnel would not let me near the car. Hugh was being cut out of the front seat. Jenny was hit by the trunk of the car as it flew up from the impact. Jenny was dead. I was in shock, watching and crying, telling the police I knew them. I told them they were on the way to my salon. News reporters on the scene began to take my story of Jenny and Hugh. I was numb as I walked home. I was so relieved they were my only appointment for the day.

In a couple of days, I received a phone call from the family, asking me to please come to their home to see Hugh. He was still in shock, and the family was hoping that if he saw me, he might respond to me. I went to their home, feeling both guilt and sorrow. If they had not been on their way to my Salon, then Jenny would still be alive, I thought. As I walked into the house, Hugh saw me and began to cry. "Oh, kid, we almost made it there. She's gone, Donna." Finally, Hugh broke down and cried, his family by his side comforting him. I noticed he had shards of glass on top of his scalp and dried blood matted in his hair. The family said a local hospital sent him home that way, and they needed someone to help take out the glass. I replied I would help them. I went home to retrieve my supplies and returned to spray warm water on his head and remove the dried blood and the glass. I cut Hugh's hair so he would look his best for Jenny's funeral. I drove ninety-eight miles one way to attend the memorial, taking Jenny's favorite pie along for the family. It took me a few weeks to pray through the feelings of false guilt, but it lifted off my emotions with the counsel of friends and Jenny's family. I took great comfort in knowing Jenny had made her peace with God, and I will see her when I get to heaven too.

Another lady, named Louise, also came to my salon for several years. Both Louise and her husband, Chuck, were in their eighties, and I found them to be a very interesting couple. They would come together about every three months when Louise needed a perm.

They believed in [4]metaphysics. I would tell them many stories of God's love to me, and they listened politely to each one. Chuck was not happy because I didn't vote for his political party, but he figured I was still okay in his book. One day, while backing out of my driveway, he hit and smashed my mailbox. He was so angry about it he actually went home and called his attorney. He would tell me years later he just knew I was going to file a lawsuit against him because I was one of *those Christians*. Chuck waited for years, and no lawsuit ever came. When he questioned me about it later, once again, he was angry that I had not filed the lawsuit. I told Chuck I never even considered such a thing! He was also angry because I fixed the mailbox on my own. He was baffled; he thought he knew it all.

Slowly Chuck began to trust me, and he would occasionally come in with Louise and sit for our conversations. One day Chuck called me and said that Louise would not be coming for her appointment. She was sick and could I please just come and sit with her because she felt peace in my presence. Now, I knew whose presence she was really feeling when I was around her, but she refused to hear the name of Jesus Christ. I went to their home to visit with her and tried to talk to her about Jesus but to no avail. In two weeks, Chuck called to tell me Louise was in the hospital and had suffered a severe heart attack.

I asked the Lord if I should go see her, and I felt a big yes in my heart. The Lord also told me she had died in the aid car and saw demons and was scared. I called several friends to have them pray for me during my visit with Louise. As I drove to the hospital, I asked God to have everyone leave the room, especially Chuck, so

[4] "Metaphysics is a division of philosophy that is concerned with the fundamental nature of reality and being. It investigates the nature of reality apart from the existence of God. It seeks to understand the origin and meaning of everything through thought alone." (Wikipedia)

I could talk honestly to Louise alone. When I entered the room, Chuck *just decided* to go for a walk, and their son *just decided* to return his rental car. I pulled up a chair and began to talk to her. This is what I said, "Louise, do you know who I am?" She replied yes, she knew it was Donna. I told her she was dying and that God had sent me to talk to her. He also revealed to me she had died in the aid car and had seen demons. The look on her face told me she was shocked into listening to me as never before. I told her Jesus came for her too, and she needed forgiveness for her sins so she could go into His heaven when she died. I told her that if she refused, then the demons would return again and take her with them. She was very willing at that moment to repeat the sinner's prayer I led her in. Tears streamed down her face as she said, "Oh thank you, Jesus."

Louise died a few days later, and I was so thankful for the years I had spent doing her hair and walking her in and out of the salon on my arm due to her bad back. Chuck called me several times after his wife passed away. He allowed me to pray for him after I listened to him say how much he missed Louise. I knew his pain from personal experience.

I met a very sweet elderly couple who were retired ministers. Matthew and Clara loved their cherry red sports car. They took country rides, holding hands like young lovers. I was invited to their renewal of vows and watched as Clara was walked down the aisle on her son's arm, Matthew grinning at her from the front. He sang a love song to her with his well-aged voice. There was not a dry eye in the church.

One day Clara told me Matthew had been diagnosed with Alzheimer disease. She cried in my shop and asked me to pray that God would take them both home together. She had fifty years with Matthew and the thought of life without him was unbearable. We agreed in prayer as her perm was processing. Cotton and rods and a plastic bag didn't stop us from approaching the throne room of God. The family took the car keys away from them and they were very sad about it. But they must have hidden a set someplace because shortly after this I saw them once again in that cherry red sports car driving down the road near my house. He had his arm resting on the window with a big grin on his face.

The prayer that Clara and I prayed was answered because within a year she passed away. Matthew never knew she had died because his memory was gone. I attended the memorial service. The family didn't know me because our relationship was in the salon only. I took a special card and wrote several comments on how they had spoken of their children with great love.

This precious couple had been a blessing to me as a single mom, they had poured out so much of God's love on me during a simple hair cut appointment. The Holy Spirit had led them to my shop. It reminded me of the times when Jesus baked fish and bread for his disciples on the shore. Such simple and practical love, God style.

There were many times of laughter in Personal Touch Hair salon. I had a surprise party for Sarah down in that space and turned it over to her friends to do make overs on each other. It became a prayer room as well as a place to meet for mentoring young women who were at a cross roads in their young lives. On my walls hung many gifts from people who came in to be refreshed in their hearts and minds. It was an oasis of God's love and a place of joy.

PERSONAL REFLECTION

When the salon was being built, I stood by the new door singing and praying as I dedicated the space to the glory of God. There were many times when a divine anointing was evident in the salon through the numerous opportunities I had to minister to my customers. I am so thankful God trusted me with these ladies and with so many others who came in during the time I was in business.

It was on-the-job training for the years ahead, and every day the carnation was being formed.

In 2017, my husband removed the signpost from my yard. It had been there for many years. As it fell down and was cut up, I reflected on all the destroyed signs, the customers, and the times of ministry I experienced at Personal Touch Hair Salon. I felt a door had softly closed within me. "Thank you, Lord, for blessing me in that small business place downstairs.

I have met other sisters in Christ who also have a hair salon like mine. The Lord has many places filled with his glory as his sons and daughters allow him to use them in everyday life. You are an amazing God!"

And whoever gives one of these little ones only a
cup of cold water in the name of a disciple,
assuredly, I say to you, he shall by no means lose his reward.
—Matthew 10:42 (NKJV)

CHAPTER 48

MAKING AMENDS

As shared in an earlier chapter, "A New Church and a New Season," I was now attending a new church. When I left my former church, I was angry and frustrated. I did not say very many goodbyes. I was just suddenly gone. I did not realize my abrupt departure hurt people, but God knew it did.

A couple of years earlier, I became involved at a local home for women. I gave the ladies in the program free hair care. I also became friends with the leadership. One of the counselors told me the ministry needed a new church to attend, so I invited them to my old church. A new class was forming for single, young adults, and the teachers were former ministers. They had a sincere concern for the young adults attending the church. I received a call from them and was told I would be coming to the class to be a mentor type person since I was at least ten years older than the others attending. I knew these ministers loved me and wanted me to feel needed. I appreciated their concern and agreed to come and help in the class.

I was able to extend an invitation to all of the ladies, counselors, and others from the home for women to come. We loved the class and the unity that formed between us. We had several activities for fellowship, and the class grew to thirty people. But the church drama in the leadership spilled over onto the class, and due to jealousy, the class was cancelled. The pastor and his wife were fearful that the former ministers who led the class might try to take over the church. Not true!

Following this event, I left and began to attend my new church. Eventually I lost contact with the home for women. I was also busy with my parents, who had come to live with me. Dad was dying of heart disease and cancer; my time was not my own. I had to lend a hand and a heart to my mom, who was Dad's main caregiver.

A time came when I was learning about spiritual warfare at my new church. I had a deep desire to share with others about our authority in Jesus and the power of God to set those held captive in oppression and bondage free. I was waking up to who I truly was as a Christian, and God had given me the gift of teaching. I had a desire to teach all of my friends about spiritual warfare.

My friend Theresa was the secretary at the home for women. She asked me if I would consider coming to help pray for one of the ladies new to the program. Evidently this lady was being tormented by demons in her sleep. She had given herself over to drugs and a dark lifestyle before she came there. I agreed to go. I received the blessing of my church leadership at Clover Creek to do this and began to pray about the appointment a week before my visit. There were to be four other staff women from the women's home who would pray with me. I knew all them from my former church.

On the day of the meeting, I headed out with an attitude of dependence on God and a deep desire to see this woman set free. As I drove up the winding driveway, the Holy Spirit began to speak to me: "Donna, before you pray for this woman today, you need to make amends. You did not say goodbye, and these women you are praying with were deeply wounded by your actions."

Now God did not say I was wrong to leave the church, but I did not close that door in a God-honoring way. We were going to enter into some powerful prayer, and the wounds had to be exposed and healed by my apology first. This would bring a powerful unity and a love between all of us.

When I arrived, I obeyed the Lord's direction. I felt excited to speak to them and tell them what God had said. I apologized for abruptly leaving the church they still attended. They were surprised when I asked for forgiveness for my attitude and said that I was sorry I had hurt them. Tears fell, and we embraced each other. The presence of the Holy Spirit was thick and sweet in the room. Each woman asked me to lay hands upon her. I prayed a blessing on each one as the Holy Spirit gave me the words. God's peace flooded the room. Now we were ready to face the warfare ahead of us.

The prayer time began, and the woman we were ministering to refused to repent of the anger she had against God. She was blaming Him for the consequences of her own decisions while in her former lifestyle. No words or scriptures would reach her heart. She had convinced herself that God had let her down. We could only encourage her to continue to seek God for freedom and asked Him to reveal truth to her. Unfortunately, she did not open her heart to the mighty counselor during our ministry time with her.

PERSONAL REFLECTION

There was good fruit from that prayer time at the women's home. Sisters and friends were forgiven and restored by the Lord. We are still in contact, and there is a bond between us that will not be broken.

Can two walk together, unless they are agreed?
—Amos 3:3 (NKJV)

CHAPTER 49

THE STORY OF JAN

In this story, I'm sharing with you how God gave me a love for a woman I would meet in a most unusual way. I needed an increase of true godly compassion, and this experience you're about to read helped me immensely.

So here we go!

I went to my doctor because I was having digestive problems. He referred me to a specialist who prescribed a barium enema. I am a very modest woman, and this test was not on my bucket list of things to do. My first response was a flat no thanks, but I finally made up my mind to get it done. On the day of my appointment, I argued with myself and with God all the way to the specialty center. But then I figured I could do just about anything for thirty minutes, and I wouldn't know the people there and would never see them again. I comforted myself with this perspective, put on the infamous medical gown, and sat on the cold table waiting for the person who would give me the barium enema.

The door opened, and in came one of the tallest and largest women I had ever seen. Now, I am not small, but she was at least six feet three inches and about three hundred pounds. She was friendly and introduced herself as Jan. She turned to read my chart and suddenly gasped and said to me, "You're Donna Gurth. Oh my goodness! I am so glad to meet you!" She proceeded to tell me she attended my church. My stomach greeted my toes at that moment.

She went on to say she knew I was a widow, had two kids, and even lived down the street from her. She then said she had read about me in the church bulletin and was praying to meet me. She was thrilled I was here. Then she said, "I am going to give you your barium enema today." I cannot explain to you, dear reader, what my thoughts were at the moment, except that I was having a very serious conversation with God.

As she began the process, the doctor entered the room and watched the monitor as the barium entered my body. It was drained out, more barium was put in, and the table was tilted up and down to be sure it covered all my insides. The whole time this was going on, Jan was spilling out her life story and asking me for personal council. Good grief! The doctor, observing all of this, asked us if we knew each other. Jan informed the doctor, "No, we just met." Then she said, "God has just answered my prayer and sent Donna in to meet me!" She continued to talk to me throughout the appointment, and to be honest with you, I did not care to have a conversation at that moment! I felt invaded.

I wanted my clothes and my car right now! I wanted ten miles between Jan and me, and I certainly didn't want to ever see her again. My pride was tied up in knots, and I wanted to scream and cry all at once. Jan's parting words were that she knew I was a table leader at the upcoming Bible study at our church and that she planned to sit at my table. Oh, joy!

The week following my medical test, I actually began to laugh about the whole event, but I still did not want to see Jan again. The day of the Bible study came, and true to her promise, she showed up and sat at my table. She smiled at me and said, "I can't wait to tell the other ladies how I met you!" I firmly told her that she was *not* going to mention it to anyone else! A new support group for women who wanted to take some weight off was also starting at my home. And, yes, Jan showed up at my house for that group as well. I could not get away from this woman, and I was beginning to get the impression the Lord was putting her in my face for a reason.

About six months after the original meeting with Jan, I received a phone call that answered this question. It happened on a Saturday as I was finishing up my final customer in the salon. On the other end of the phone was a nurse calling from Virginia Mason Hospital in Seattle. The nurse told me Jan was admitted into the ICU with a malignant brain tumor. None of her family would come to visit her. She had gone blind and was asking for me. I told the nurse I was on my way. I quickly set off for Seattle to try to find Virginia Mason Hospital and Jan.

After getting lost and going to the wrong hospital, I finally arrived. Jan heard my voice as I was talking to the nurse, and she began to call out for me. I was very shocked to see her forehead sunk in. In just a few short days, she looked completely different. I brought my Bible and read Psalm 91 to her, anointed her with oil, and prayed over her. I promised I would return the next day and bring my daughter, Sarah, with me. I found my attitude had taken a different turn with Jan, and I repented to God for my pride and arrogance in my past dealings with her. She gave me her house key to look after her dogs. I was mopping up dog urine, cleaning up her messes, and encouraging her at the hospital daily.

Surgery was scheduled to try to remove the tumor, and she asked me to give her a haircut lying in the hospital bed. I came armed with my supplies, and we had fun laughing in the face of a very serious situation. One of her friends made her a prairie bonnet style hat to cover the surgery scar. They could only remove a small section of the tumor, just enough to give her back a little eyesight for a season. The cancer was aggressive, and she knew her time was limited. Her peaceful and accepting attitude was a lesson for me, and it had a deep and permanent impact.

On one of my visits to the hospital, Jan was eating lunch when I arrived. She began to laugh because here stood her diet group leader. Sitting on her lunch tray was a giant cheeseburger, a pile of fries, a large piece of chocolate cake, and a piece of pie to boot! Jan also ordered a milkshake to wash it all down. Looking up at me, Jan said, "I find this scenario funny. Here you are my diet group leader, watching me pig out, and I don't care one bit. I'm going to die anyway, so I'm going to eat whatever I want." I smiled at her and said, "Knock yourself out, my friend. Enjoy every bite."

After Jan came home from the hospital, Sarah and I picked her up each Sunday for church, and she squeezed herself into my little Toyota. Jan wore that prairie hat everywhere she went with us. She had to use a cane and kept her hand on my shoulder. I led my partially blind friend into the church and found a chair for her beside me. One Sunday morning, Jan plowed into one of the ushers on her way to the restroom. He didn't know she was partially blind and she couldn't see him standing there. This big 6'3" woman knocked him flat on the floor.

One Friday morning, she needed to be in North Seattle by 6:00 a.m. Since I was my own boss, I rearranged my schedule and drove her to the appointment. That morning, on the I-5 freeway, the traffic was awful. Jan talked my ear off as I kept my eye on the road. Suddenly I heard in my spirit a warning, "Watch your right front." As soon as I looked, a car veered over toward us. I had just enough time to get out of the way. I knew the Lord had given His angels charge over us, and they were doing their job well.

After her treatment, we left for home. Jan wanted to take me to her favorite restaurant in Auburn for lunch, so we headed in that direction. She fell asleep in the front seat before we arrived. Now, as I said, she was a very large woman, and the medication she was now taking made her swell up, adding even more to her size. Her upper chest was now lying on my dashboard, and she had on the prairie bonnet. Her mouth was wide open, and she was snoring just as I got off the exit before the restaurant.

Suddenly a large, black, highway monster truck came to a stop beside us. The look on the face of the man in the truck was priceless! Jan woke up to see him looking at her with his mouth gaping in unbelief. Jan smiled and waved at him in time for the red light to change, and he left behind hot rubber tracks as he blasted out of there. The laughter began with Jan as we realized what that poor guy must have thought. It was one crazy day!

It was not long until Jan began noticing her eyes were getting worse and she needed to make her funeral arrangements as soon as possible while she could still see. Now, I had buried my husband at the same memorial park Jan selected. Every time I drove by, I would feel a deep ache inside my soul because of all the painful memories it brought. God was about to change that and heal another level of my pain.

I reluctantly agreed to go with Jan to help her plan for the disposal of her body. We were ushered into the exact same room where I had been for Dave's arrangements. The same man who helped me during that time was the person who came to meet Jan. Mark recognized me and said it was nice to see me again. The feelings were not mutual, but I nodded my head politely. Jan was told to go the adjoining room to pick out the urn she wanted for her ashes. It was the same room where I had made my painful decisions many years earlier. It was as if I was revisiting a scene from my past in preparation for God's healing touch.

After careful consideration, Jan chose a very beautiful but tall container with a long-stem red rose engraved on it. As she filled out the paperwork and answered all of the questions, Mark asked her which urn she had chosen. Jan pointed to her choice and was quickly told she would not be able to use her carefully chosen urn.

Jan took a deep breath, and with anger, she began to yell, "Do you mean to tell me that after living my entire life being too big for the clothes I wanted to wear, and too big for the car I wanted, and now that I am dying and you're going to burn my body, that I am still too big for the urn I want?"

The look on Mark's face was priceless as he sheepishly said, "Oh no, ma'am, that's not an urn; that's a flower vase!" The laughter that broke out around the table was wonderful! I am sure the employees of the memorial home had not heard such a roll of laughter coming from that room before. God had given me a new memory to replace a tough one. Now when I drive by, I giggle, thinking about the urn that was a flower vase.

Sarah and I visited Jan at the nursing home the final week of her life. Though completely blind now, she still knew who we were. We prayed over her, asking God to have mercy on her and take her home. The final words I heard from Jan were, "I see the *Titanic* outside my window, and I need to get on board."

PERSONAL REFLECTION

God sure does some great things, and He teaches us so much through the many issues of life. I am so glad He used Jan to rub off some of the hard edges on my attitude and immensely deepen my compassion. Many times, through her illness she would look at me and say with confidence, "One day, Donna, you are going to speak to many women." Jan knew very little of the story of my life, but I have pondered her comments. They are on the back burner of my mind, simmering like a good pot of homemade soup.

And be kind to one another, tenderhearted,
forgiving one another, even as God in Christ forgave you.
—Ephesians 4:32 (NKJV)

CHAPTER 50

OUTSIDE OF MY LITTLE BOX

One morning I received a phone call that would alter my heart and change me very deeply. I had lived a life protected from the hurts and needs of others, and God wanted to broaden my perspective once again. On the other end of the call was a friend from church. She asked me this question, "Donna, how many hours a month do you want to give free haircuts at our church's ministry to the homeless?" I didn't recall volunteering for this assignment, but Cindy would not take no for an answer. I told her I could come once a month and see how that worked. So the next adventure began.

I was afraid to mingle with this group of people and didn't know what to expect. I began by hiding my purse in the workroom and started with small talk that was completely impersonal. For the next few months, I began to develop a soft place inside my heart for the less fortunate. I met sweet children, and I heard so many stories of tragedy from the people to whom I gave haircuts. Don't get me wrong; I also heard many stories with the blame game and entitlement issues as well. But, by far, most of the people I met found a place in my heart.

Before long, I began to attend their Sunday church service and volunteered to join the kitchen crew. My friend Brenda and

I cooked a meal to feed about eighty-five to a hundred people one Sunday each month. We didn't have a stove, so everything was cooked in two or three eighteen-quart roasters. We didn't know month to month what we were making, but we prayed in both the food and the people to help out. Desserts were donated by a local bakery from their excess. Nevertheless, Brenda and I were good cooks, and we wanted to provide something special for them. Many times, we added to the menu from our own resources. To hand a hot bowl of food to a cold and hungry person ministered to us in ways we had never known before. Seeing the provision of God once again in a different venue was downright fun.

One Sunday we cooked diced ham and gravy but had nothing to pour it over. We prayed, and this is what God provided. About two hours before we were to open, a lady was getting groceries at Cash and Carry down the street. While shopping, she heard a voice tell her to buy two one-gallon cans of dried potato flakes and take them to that ministry down the street. The Lord led her to us, and she pulled up outside the kitchen door and sheepishly told us what she had heard. We thanked her and told her of our need. She drove away completely baffled, having never heard the voice of God before. It didn't take us long to get the butter and milk out of the refrigerator and get those potatoes cooked and ready to serve. I find it interesting that it took every moment of those two hours to heat the liquid in the roasters before adding the potato flakes. If it was any later than that, we would not have had enough time to prepare them. Once again, God planned it all out perfectly! The woman in charge of the kitchen only had to mention that she wanted to make potato soup for the homeless that Sunday. God heard her and sent someone in with several gallons of milk, a sack of potatoes, a slab of bacon and a huge bag of onions.

Then there was the time He provided for a volunteer appreciation barbeque. We had about eighty people coming, but we didn't have money for burgers or buns or anything else. And so we prayed! About two hours before people arrived, a call came from a local church. They just finished their barbeque and had two hundred Angus burger patties with buns and several salads left over. Could we use them? That next Thanksgiving brought four huge cooked turkeys complete with gravy and mashed potatoes. It was a blessing to receive those gifts and I am sure the giver was blessed by the Lord for their obedience.

Another story was our Easter dinner. We were teaching the people about the Passover meal. But we needed meat for the special dinner we were serving. The Lord sent us two legs of lamb, which was enough to feed our crowd. God sees us, He hears us, and He loves to be involved with every detail in our lives. God has not lost his recipe for manna, he just changed his recipe for us many times.

During the three years I was there, I led a Bible study with the ladies, and several of them came into a personal relationship with Jesus Christ. I was able to cook for them, counsel them, pray for them, and give them clothing. Time after time, we saw God provide for this ministry to the homeless in amazing yet practical ways. Occasionally, I see some of the people I met there and love to give and receive their hugs.

Personal Reflection

We all need to be encouraged as we walk through this dark, troubled world. Being at this ministry melted my heart, and it showed me my many blessings. I no longer hated mowing my lawn because at least I had my own home and a lawn to mow. And I am so thankful I have a kitchen and a bed and a bathroom of my own. I am sure that you get the picture!

Truly, God does make provision for the calling and assignments He gives us. I believe this happens through the gifts of the Holy

Spirit, which are still for the church today. We had special prayer groups at my regular church, and on occasion they would minister to me through the gifts of the Holy Spirit. Here are a few of the words spoken prophetically over me by these prayer teams. Keep in mind these are words spoken to me by people I did not personally know. They were not involved in the ministry to the homeless where I was serving. Here is a list of ten things spoken over me.

1) "You have a heart of service, caring for those that are poor."
2) "I see you watering those who are thirsty, Donna."
3) "You're like a mother to those who are lost."
4) "God's love is your strength."
5) "You pour life into others who are struggling."
6) "You're compassionate and loving because your life is built upon the rock, Jesus Christ."
7) "You're a cheerleader, a counselor of truth."
8) "You love to help the helpless."
9) "You're approachable, you're a faith walker."
10) "You're a pillar, nurturing and steadfast."

I am not bragging by listing these. I do not intend to be prideful. I know very well that anything good within me has come from one source, Jesus Christ. I will never forget the depth of the pit He drew me out of. He is my source and my strength forever! The Bible tells us if we seek God, He will be found by us and will do more in us than we can imagine. Each of these prophetic statements has been repeated time and again by others. My favorite scripture is Ephesians 3:20, "Now to Him who is able to do exceedingly abundantly above all that we ask or think, according to the power that works in us" (NKJV).

I did not realize that someone else who would become very special to me in about twelve years was also doing the same type of ministry just across town. But I will save that story for another chapter, "A Twenty-Three-Year-Old Prophecy, Finally Fulfilled!"

> Give, and it will be given to you: good measure,
> pressed down, shaken together,
> and running over will be put into your bosom.
> For with the same measure that you use,
> it will be measured back to you.
> —Luke 6:38 (NKJV)

CHAPTER 51

MISSIONARY MCDONNA

For twelve years, I hosted students from both Japan and South Korea in my home. My children and I enjoyed being involved in introducing these precious students to American culture. I had a total of twelve students over a twelve-year period. In this chapter, I will tell you about a few of them.

Aiko was a sweet Japanese girl; she was sixteen years of age. She came to spend three weeks with us the year after Dave's death. She was absolutely gorgeous and quiet. Aiko was convinced she was ugly. Her father told her she would never marry because she was not as pretty as her sister, but we found her to be very beautiful both inside and out! We could only speak to her in limited English, and I used a Japanese/American dictionary with pictures to talk to her. Aiko was especially attentive to Sarah, and I loved the sweet fellowship between them.

I always put a basket of snack food in the bedroom of my students. They studied long into the night, and I knew they would get hungry. Aiko heard that American Christians always passed the basket. She thought I was taking up an offering of snack foods because, after all, there was a basket in her room. She would add to the basket daily, and I saw that it was growing in size. The mystery ended when her Japanese high school chaperone asked me about the basket. Aiko asked her to speak to me about it. No more snack offerings were given after that, but she did empty it out a little at a time.

When Aiko returned to Japan, she cried, burying her head in my shoulder, and waved at us until we were out of sight. I received several letters from her over a six-month period. Her father told her to stop writing to me; her emotions were too tender, and it was time for her to put her visit in the past. Her final letter was to say she loved our family and goodbye forever. I still think about Aiko and pray for her.

Akihiko was a very tall and handsome Japanese teenage boy. He and Martin were the same age and size. They became friends quickly and began to compete with fishing and video games. Akihiko bought an American flag T-shirt just like the one Martin had, and he wore it almost every day. One day Akihiko asked me, "What is a taco? I hear, but I do not know what is taco?" I told him we would have tacos for dinner when he got home from his culture classes that evening. We watched as Akihiko ate six huge tacos at dinner. He dumped at least a third of a cup of hot sauce on each one. He was a fan of tacos now and was hoping to find them back home in Japan. I was glad I could enlighten him on this vital subject.

Each student attended church with us, and I prayed for them as I prayed for my own children each night before bed. The students thought this was a strange American tradition. I also kissed my kids on their cheek before bed, and Akihiko was no exception. After all, he was here to learn our way of life. When Akihiko left us, I took him to the airport, and as he backed up the ramp to the jet, he held up his ticket as if to tear it in half. He said to us, "I stay in American and be Gurth family number-two son!" I truly did want to keep him! But I told him his mother would not be very happy with him if he stayed.

We received several letters from Akihiko, and he told me I had given him his first kiss. Poor guy! He also said American girls were very womanly. Many years later, I found him on Facebook. The reaction he had was sweet. He typed online "Wow, my American mother, Wow, twenty-five years later!" He showed me pictures of his wife and children. He is a fine businessman today. My family has sweet memories of Akihiko.

Se Jun was only eleven years old when he arrived at our home. He had been awake for over twenty-four hours and was at the end of his endurance. Now, we had a dog in the house as a pet, and from what I had studied, in South Korea, his home, dogs were used as meat. Se Jun screamed and ran back out to the car when he saw our dog, Caleb. I can only imagine his thoughts. *This crazy woman has meat running around her house!* But within a few days, Se Jun was holding Caleb and teasing Sarah about his legs making good barbeque!

Another eleven-year-old South Korean boy came to us at the same time. His name was Tae Min. This young man was not as fearful. He was watching and listening to everything that was new around him. When we came inside the house, I took both him and Se Jun to the guest bedroom they would share. I talked with them through a Korean/English dictionary. Later, when it was dinnertime, I could not find Se Jun. I discovered him in the upstairs bathroom crying, blowing his nose on the guest towels. I touched his shoulder as if to say it was going to be okay; he jerked away from me in fear. I had to do something to reassure them both. I called a friend from church named Sook. She was Korean and came here with her American husband. I knew she would help me. Through her interpretation, I told both boys they were in a safe place and we were glad to have them. Sook joined us for dinner, and the boys seemed very relaxed after she left. I took the boys down to their room and told them it was bedtime. I prayed over them, and they folded their hands in honor. They both said a loud "Amen" when I finished. I had a suspicion they were from Christian homes.

I heard noises a few hours later, and I peeked into the room to see them playing a game and laughing together. In the morning, I went down to wake them up to discover they had both made their beds on the floor and were wrapped up in their blankets like little burritos. For breakfast, I decided to prepare hot rice, chicken, and Kim Chee. I thought it would please them. A little taste of home, right? Wrong! They told me they would like Coco Pebbles! How in the world did they know about that cereal? I went through four boxes of Coco Pebbles and lots of bananas during their stay.

Se Jun's parents called me from South Korea. They used a translator from his private school. They wanted to thank me for taking their son. I discovered they were Christians too and had prayed God would place their son in a Christian home during his American home stay. It was a precious time talking with them as I heard the joy in their voices.

Tae Min had trouble getting out of bed every morning. His father called early one morning and asked me if he got up on the first wakeup call. When I told him that he did not until I made him, his father was not happy. He told me, "You must discipline my son!" After putting Tae Min on the phone with his father, he was obviously upset. The next morning, Tae Min got out of bed on my first call. His father phoned us again a few days later and was happy to hear his son was now obedient.

While driving home one evening after the culture classes, both boys spotted the golden arches of McDonalds. They were very excited as they pointed and whined and convinced me to buy them dinner at the golden arches. They both had a full meal, a large-sized Big Mac dinner as well as chicken nuggets and a milkshake. I was surprised to see them eat so much. The next night they tried to convince me to return to McDonalds. I took them home and surprised them with home-cooked cheeseburgers—I mean really huge burgers—along with homemade french fries. After they saw what I had prepared for them, they began to call me McDonna. That became my nickname until the day they returned to South Korea.

I found Se Jun on Facebook a few years ago. We have communicated online several times. I learned he was on his own, lonely, and without a church home in his city. It just so happened that a friend of mine was in his city for several evangelical meetings. I got the name and address of this church for Se Jun. He has attended with a friend and likes the church. They will help Se Jun in his life to become the person God created him to be.

The final student I will mention was from Tokyo, Japan. Her name is Nanami, and she is a critical care nurse. She came to us to learn the American culture and improve her English-speaking skills. Nanami was twenty-six years old and very sweet. She was excited to see she had her own room and a bathroom to herself. This was a luxury she did not have at home. Not long after her arrival, she came to me to ask a question. "You are a single woman with a business and a daughter, but you have no stress. Why?" Oh, how I wished I could speak fluent Japanese! I tried my best to use the Japanese/English dictionary to convey to her my testimony of Jesus Christ and His peace. I could see God was doing something in her.

Not long after this, Nanami asked to go with me to a ladies' retreat at my church. I asked a few of the single women her age who were also going to include her as part of their group. They were all very willing to have her join them. After the weekend was over, Nanami came to me and said, "I feel it, I see, I understand." I asked Nanami if she would like to receive Jesus as her Savior. Her response was that her family had a traditional religion. But I could see that Jesus was working within her heart.

One of the things every student wanted to do was to teach me how to cook some of their favorite foods from their country. We were also invited to a few homes for dinner. The women in these homes were either Japanese or Korean. They were excited to visit with the students and told me I was a missionary to their countries. At each home, I noticed every time we had dinner, they had a single bowl of potato salad in the center of the table surrounded by their cultural foods. I finally asked about it and was told every American family had potato salad for every meal every day. No amount of talking would convince them otherwise.

I received an invitation to take Nanami to a local Japanese Christian church on Sunday. I was very glad to do that because I wanted her to hear the gospel of Jesus Christ in her language from her own people. I was the one and only tall white woman in a crowd of two hundred. I was given a special earpiece to be able to hear an English translation of the sermon. The pastor was teaching on the Good Shepherd. Perfect! Nanami did not receive Jesus that day, but many precious seeds of the gospel were planted in her soul. After the service, a precious lady literally took my arm and pulled me down the hallway. She told me I was a special guest for lunch with the pastor because I was a missionary! I tried to correct her, telling her I was only a host mother, but she would not accept my response. She told me firmly, "No, you are a missionary, and you must eat!" There, on the table, were huge platters of unrecognizable foods with potato salad in the middle!

The seven months of her visit came to an end, and Nanami asked me to drive her to the airport. She did not want to take the bus with the younger students returning home; she wanted to be alone with me. That was the toughest goodbye. Nanami had become my daughter, and I loved her. I took her face in my hands and said, "Nanami, Jesus speaks Japanese!" She smiled at me and buried her face in my shoulders before she turned to walk down the aisle to the jet. I have never found her on Facebook.

My salon became a gathering place for the students living with other host families in the area. One girl bleached her black hair blonde, only to have her mother tell her not to return home unless her hair was black again. In a panic, she purchased one box of black hair dye and turned her bleached hair a nice shade of pea green. That was when McDonna received a 911 hair call. I had fun fixing the problem as she and her friend chatted in Japanese as I worked. She returned home to her happy mother with jet-black hair. She sent me a nice card and said I would always be her American mother and she loved me.

PERSONAL REFLECTION

I know that God had a purpose for every single student I hosted; all twelve of them felt His presence in my home. One student named Chinami said to me the day after her arrival, "You trust in an invisible God, but I trust in me!" Once again I got out my dictionary and replied to her comment. Jesus uses it all. He sees every one of my former houseguests. They each helped open my eyes to God's purpose for all of humankind.

Be hospitable to one another without grumbling.
As each one has received a gift,
minister it to one another, as good stewards
of the manifold grace of God.
—1 Peter 4:9–10 (NKJV)

Foreign students with Gurth family

CHAPTER 52

THE WEDDING GIFT

My son, Martin, was soon to be married. The couple chose a Christmas wedding theme, and we set about preparing for the special day. My dad had a difficult time leaving the house, as his cancer and heart problems limited him physically. So the vows were to be shared in my living room in front of the fireplace with the immediate family surrounding the young couple.

As the day approached, I knew in my heart that Martin was missing his dad. The sense of loss was evident. I had been thinking about it every day, but I could not do anything to fill up the void I knew my son was sensing ... but God had a plan. Two weeks before Martin's wedding day, I awoke in the early hours of the morning. The Lord reminded me of a poem of love Dave had written to Martin on the final Valentine's Day before he died. I got out of bed and was led to a particular photo album and found the poem without a problem. I had forgotten about that poem, but God knew right where it was!

I felt impressed to go to Walmart the next day to look for a particular frame and also to find three other pictures of Martin and Dave together at different times that created special memories. I was to add these photos to the frame with scripture scrapbook stickers and sensed the Lord telling me to wrap it up in wedding gift paper. The Lord let me know that Martin would arrive early on the day of his wedding and that he would be grieving for Dave and would visit the grave just before coming to my house.

I obeyed the Lord's prompting and prepared the gift just as directed. True to what the Lord had revealed to me, Martin arrived early. He had been crying, and I told him I knew where he had been. I asked him to come to my room because I had something for him. As I gave the gift to him, I let him know it was from his dad and God and how I had been directed to make it for him. God knew his heart and what he would need on his wedding day. Martin stared at the wedding gift for a moment and then said, "Mom, you have no idea how much this means to me."

Personal Reflection

I could always kiss Martin's "owies" away as a child. But now he was a man, and this one was too deep; I could not ease the pain. It took our heavenly Father's loving compassion to heal this wound. He always knows how to meet our deepest needs. Today this special gift hangs on the wall in Martin and Sheri's home, a testimony of God's compassionate heart.

On this special day, I quietly looked at my children and reflected on how far they had come since the death of their beloved daddy. We had been through so much as we grieved, prayed, and lived our lives believing that God was with us. Indeed, when we passed through the waters of loss, we were not overcome! We were whole once again, healed and happy. We were now a family of four with a new daughter joining us. We keep that boat of faith with us and choose to stay in it, with Jesus always at the helm.

And God will wipe away every tear from their
eyes; there shall be no more death, nor sorrow,
nor crying. There shall be no more pain,
for the former things have passed away.
—Revelation 21:4 (NKJV)

Martin and Sheri Gurth at Seahawks game

CHAPTER 53

THE BUILDING OF A STRONGHOLD— HOW TO BATTLE THE BULGE

This chapter is by far the hardest one for me to write. I can only guess that is because of how deep the roots have grown within my soul and how much shame and hurt it has caused me in my life. Some wounds need more time to heal than others, and this is one of those wounds. The tug-of-war between my fleshly appetite for food and my desire to be normal and healthy has been a long and hard-fought war.

I know, dear readers, there are a countless number of you reading this book who can identify and yearn for an answer to your own battle with the stronghold I am going to talk about now. So let me begin my story!

As a little girl, I loved my grandma Josie. She was from Kentucky, complete with the bun in her hair, granny shoes, her homemade aprons, and wired glasses. Her warm hugs and firm spankings somehow comforted me. Boy, could she cook and eat! That equaled love to me. Grandma Josie lived with our family for eighteen months when I was quite young. Her favorite meal to cook was homegrown green beans simmered in bacon and grease, onions and tiny red potatoes. Then she added hot cornbread with lots of melted butter, vine ripe tomatoes, and cold cottage cheese. I was in love!

Grandma Josie would clean the kitchen and hum a simple phrase, "Doe dee doe dee doe," and repeat it over as she cleaned. If we had eaten salad for dinner, she would save the final few bites and let it sit in the refrigerator until just before bedtime. Smoothing butter over a piece of bread, she would dip it in the wilted salad and eat with pleasure. I would stand by her rocking chair and hear the sounds of her false teeth clattering as she chewed. Once in a while, she would give me a tiny bite. That was love to me, and I wanted more!

When I was about four years old, Grandma Josie moved back to Kentucky to remarry, and I missed her terribly. So I turned my attention to watching my parents eat. Don't ask me why; it was just an inner craving, a deeply planted pleasure within me. Mom was quite a good cook, and boy could she make amazing spaghetti sauce. Mom would serve us kids first. Then she and Dad would sit down to eat together. On occasion, I would watch, hearing the sounds of food being eaten with pleasure, watching Dad butter one piece of bread after another and soak up the sauce that would form from the little bit of water from the noodles mixed with the sauce. Oh, wow, I was in love. And the cravings and the addiction grew deeper.

We had a generational stronghold of alcoholism on Dad's side of the family. In the hills of Kentucky, my grandfather Arberry was a bootlegger. He had my dad deliver the booze to his customers. Dad decided to drain off some for his own use, and over time he formed an addiction that would destroy so much of what he loved. When Dad was born again, the Lord mercifully took that addiction away from him. The seeds of it were planted in me, but instead of alcohol, it vented itself with an obsession for food.

In 1966, in Fairbanks, Alaska, I was sitting with my parents at church. It was a Sunday evening, and we had just finished a potluck fellowship time. After the worship service, we sat down to hear the preaching when suddenly I was aware of something unseen standing behind me. I felt an overwhelming urge to tell my mother I had to use the bathroom, but instead I sneaked downstairs to get a piece of leftover chicken. I obeyed that prompting; hiding in the bathroom, I ate the chicken with great delight. Each bite was soothing, very addictive, and it was fun because I was doing it in secret!

The stronghold pushed deeper inside my soul. I began to think about lunchtime at school instead of recess. I even became a lunch helper so I could enjoy being near the kitchen and maybe get a larger serving. One day in junior high, I got caught spooning bites of leftover Spanish rice into my mouth. I was embarrassed and said something like, "Oh, I dropped a dime in it and need to find it." I was just sure she believed that one! And the stronghold grew deeper. I could not shake the inner compulsion to eat, to eat often, and to eat more than I needed ... especially spaghetti!

We had a flood in Fairbanks in 1968, and we were forced to stay out of town with an employee of my dad's. The final week we were there, all the women put together one huge pot of soup from whatever they could find. I stood in front of that pot and watched it cook. I was fearful because we had no more food in the house and there were eight other people staying there. Fear would come and then subside again and again all through my young years. It was always present deep within me and resurrected itself during times of trauma. I only learned to kill the fear as it rose up in my later years.

When I was a teenager, I discovered that if I "diet," the fat will go away. I became very good at counting calories. But that inner drive was stronger than my desire to be thin and pretty. People said, "Oh, Donna, you have such a pretty face." You know the drill— hint, hint, get the fat off, girl! All that did was make me angry; why was my acceptance based on my size? So I rebelled!

One night my dad decided to weigh me in front of my entire family. The number shocked us all, but I was angry and so embarrassed I wanted to run away. I felt rejected and laughed at, not good enough once again. And now rebellion was added to the food addiction. I began to form a strong resistance to anyone's comments that I should lose weight. I could not find clothing that fit me. I avoided every mirror and pretended I did not care. But I did care. I was just stuck in bondage! In church, we didn't call it bondage; we avoided the issue and we enjoyed our potluck dinners. It was the acceptable form of addiction, and my girdle got tighter after every feast. A spirit of gluttony had attached itself to my soul.

I met a guy in high school who I began to have feelings for. So that became my motivation to lose some weight. But my agenda was to capture his heart. Even after losing a large amount of weight, my agenda failed, so food became my love once again. I remember making a vow that once I had my own kitchen, I was going to cook and eat as much as I wanted, and nobody would stop me. I even had a hope chest full of kitchen supplies as I dreamed about my favorite place in my future house. The bullying all through school was pretty intense. And it did not stop there; it continued at church. I felt rejected and mocked. There was no safe place for me; even my so-called close friends were often unfaithful and joined the mockers. I just retreated deeper inside myself.

My family moved to Juneau, Alaska, and I became busy with a job. I dropped a chunk of weight without meaning to and was getting a lot of attention from men. The drive toward food was gone for a period of time, and I began dating Dave. After we married and I realized I had a kitchen of my own, the drive resurrected itself. Boy, did I cook! I still craved spaghetti because I was looking for that familiar childhood comfort. We both gained a large amount of weight the first year of our marriage, and we were miserable. My married name was Gurth, pronounced the same as "girth," which means "circumference around." When I found this out, I was both horrified and embarrassed.

Whether I was sad, lonely, or fearful, whatever the emotion, it was a time to satisfy it with food. I became isolated from people; fear of rejection was ever present. I became deeply depressed. We made our trip to Juneau as mentioned in an earlier chapter ("I Sure Wish I Knew God Like That"), and I went into the chapel at the Shrine of St. Therese and gave myself to Jesus.

A few years later, the Lord began to speak within my spirit about temperance being a fruit of His Holy Spirit. I was unsure what that meant, but I wanted to learn. I really wanted to have temperance but did not know how to get it. I began to pray, and early one morning the Lord showed me a picture of a double-scale balance. He impressed me that if He delivered me too quickly, I would get out of balance. Then He whispered a scripture to me. I looked it up and understood His meaning.

> Little by little I will drive them out from before you,
> until you have increased, and you inherit the land.
> —Exodus 23:30 (NKJV)

God also showed me the image of a fruit tree that was propped up by small ropes on each side, firmly staked into the ground. He said that this stronghold inside of me was propped up by unseen attitudes and events of the past. As He started to deliver me, the stronghold of gluttony would grow weaker and weaker. It would take my desire for Him to work it out His way and give up all false expectations, preconceived ideas, and time frames.

I began to pray this way:

"I refuse to believe that this stronghold of food obsession is too big for You to deal with. I do not know how to deliver myself. I don't understand what this 'kingdom of lies' is composed of within me, but it's not too big for You!"

"Without Your wisdom revealed to me, I am unable to break free. My flesh is bound up, and my mind is confused by many years of slavery. I believe Your power and love will set me free!"

"I give up trying to fight this in my own strength. I quit! I will wait on You to reveal the truth and set me free!"

I would love to say that it was smooth sailing from that point, but it was not. I decided to help God out by having weight loss surgery. It did not work the first time, and it had to be redone. Then four years later, it was reversed due to health issues caused by extreme vitamin deficiency. But God was faithful, and He kept working at the inner areas that propped up this stronghold inside my soul. I had to forgive so many people, admit my own responsibility for building this stronghold, and call it what it was ... sin. I began to truly see my desire for excessive food as sin. It was a priority in me, it was my identity, and it had me!

One day I was very lonely ... I was widowed and bored. As I looked out my upstairs window, and true to the inner conditioned process of dealing with my emotions, I began to think about my amazing homemade chocolate cake recipe. I was thinking how much fun it would be to create that masterpiece, filling up the house with that wonderful aroma! I felt an excitement rise up within me! Then deep inside of me, I recognized a red flag! I knew if I made that cake, I would have more than one piece; then self-condemnation would set in, and I would end up giving it away or throwing it away. At that moment, I heard in my soul, "Feast on Me, Donna." I turned away from gazing out the window and the tantalizing fantasy cake, and I turned to my Bible, praying and feasting on Jesus. I had a terrific prayer time, and healing kept up its pace.

In my desire to help God out, I went on several diets only to fail once again and go back to the same old pattern. I was beginning to see that as long as I was going to drive this truck, I would derail

God's plans. So, I agreed with God and got into the backseat and buckled myself in; I chose to let God drive. Little by little, I saw what He was trying to show me. He put women into my life who were disciplined with eating, and I began to watch them. I also began to realize that my stomach could only hold so much. I chose to get busy, face the facts, and make myself deny the cravings. They would go away in about ten minutes. I read an article by a Christian author. She said that since you're suffering anyway, why not just suffer toward freedom? But I felt a deep sense of loss when I denied my appetite for excess food. It was painful in my emotions, but I can't feel my way into obedience and freedom. I had to obey my way into feeling good about my choice to deny my flesh. It did feel good ten minutes later, and it put a smile on my face too. It is such a slippery slope, isn't it?

It was stop and start, then stop and start again as I chose not to *diet* but to fuel my body instead. I waited longer periods between eating and gave up some of my favorite foods—fried chicken and huge amounts of pasta. Baking also had to take a very low priority in my life; it was another trap! Yes, I fell down for weeks at a time, but I got up again. Praise God! As time passed, the cravings grew less and less. I am learning to love who I am and to be comfortable in my own skin. Satan's entire strategy for my destruction was based on deception. But as God's Word says, "You are of God, little children, and have overcome them, because He who is in you is greater than he who is in the world" (1 John 4:4 NJKV).

At the writing of this story, I am down 140 pounds! Yes, that's 140 pounds! I am still battling toward the finish line of freedom, but I know God is walking me out of this stronghold. I can feel the changes inside my soul; a little here and a little there. If I could not call this bondage "my sin," I would not be freed! I have to agree with God every day, pursue temperance, and pray through each temptation. I might need to cry through it, rebuke that spirit of gluttony, wait out those ten minutes, and set my face toward obedience. This stronghold is so familiar to me. It is miserably comfortable as someone said. But God and I will win this battle for good! He doesn't wear a watch like I do. Fifty-five years of bondage takes time to die! It does not feel good, it is painful!

Then one day I saw this verse with new eyes:

> But also for this very reason, giving all diligence, add to your faith virtue, to virtue knowledge, to knowledge self-control, to self-control perseverance, to perseverance godliness, to godliness brotherly kindness, and to brotherly kindness love. For if these things are yours and abound, you will be neither barren nor unfruitful in the knowledge of our Lord Jesus Christ. For he who lacks these things is short sighted, and even to blindness, and has forgotten that he was cleansed from his old sins. (2 Peter 1:5–9 NKJV)

PERSONAL REFLECTION

The peace I have as I walk out of this stronghold is amazing. I do not want to go back to the deception of rebellion with eating. I hate self-condemnation, sorrow, self-hatred, hopelessness, and anger. All of those things came along with the package of bondage to gluttony. They have been false comforts, lies that destroy. I have seen how much of life I missed because I gave myself over to something far less. The deception of Satan in this area had grown poisonous leaves onto the carnation that was to be me! The Holy Spirit is pruning off those leaves that do not belong and uprooting every lie and obsession in my soul where I have placed food.

I was recently approached by a friend at church who showed me her eating plan. I felt rebellion and anger and resistance rise up in me. It was the same feelings that came up in me when my dad weighed me in front of the family. I chased Patricia down, and with another friend, Susan, we had an impromptu prayer time in the ladies' room ASAP because I realized those feelings had to go. They were propping up this stronghold. Being contented with myself is a new thing for me. I have to renounce false guilt, shame and self-condemning thoughts on a continual basis.

Coming into line with God's design brings peace, with each choice, one day at a time. I choose to remember that there is so much more to life than planning, shopping, cooking, and eating my creation in the kitchen. There's also so much more to life than fast-food drive-through window handouts! It's everywhere in our faces, isn't it? We have to eat, but we must manage our appetites and bring them into God's original design!

So, prune away, Holy Spirit. I will stay in the backseat, buckled up and hanging on! This is not my life. I gave it to you long ago. Do your will, my Savior and my King!

See, I have set before you today life and good, death and evil,
in that I command you today to love the Lord your God,
to walk in His ways and to keep His commandments,
His statutes, and His judgments,
that you may live and multiply; and the
Lord your God will bless you
in the land, which you go to possess.
—Deuteronomy 30:15–16 (NKJV)

Grandma Josie with husband, Elzy

CHAPTER 54

THIRTY-FIVE YEARS
OF RESENTMENT

Early one morning, at approximately 2:00 a.m., I was awakened by the Lord. I felt an inner prompting to sit up. He asked me this question, "Donna, what comes up in your heart when you think about Sean and Tom?" Well, I knew exactly what He meant. Resentment came up within me because a close family member often mentioned them in conversation. In youth group and high school, I had been made fun of by Tom. But Sean was a good friend, just as long as his buddies were not around. They had been a source of rejection and pain to me.

Yet again, God was right, and He was confronting me at 2:00 a.m. I agreed with God; I needed to deal with it. I sensed the Lord's voice in my spirit asking me, "Don't you think thirty-five years of resentment is long enough?" I said, "Well yes, that sure is, Lord." Then the Lord said, "You know what to do with this, Donna."

I began to repent for the thirty-five years of resentment, receive God's forgiveness, and then to bless both Sean and Tom. I asked the Lord to help them and provide for both of them. I felt like I had just dropped fifty pounds of sinful baggage.

I had no idea that I would see both of these men at a funeral only six weeks after my prayer time with God. I was able to approach them both and have a conversation with them. All of the resentment was gone. They were both very friendly and glad to see me. They introduced me to their families, and we later sat together for refreshments.

Personal Reflection

As I drove home that night, I told my daughter the whole story. I was amazed at how much God wants me to have a pure heart and how much damage the continued resentment was doing inside of me. It was a bitter root that had grown deep. I gave the Lord permission to search my heart and keep uprooting anything that was displeasing to Him.

Search me, O God, and know my heart;
Try me, and know my anxieties;
And see if there is any wicked way in me,
And lead me in the way everlasting.
—Psalm 139:23–24 (NKJV)

CHAPTER 55

A SPECIAL TIME OF RESTORATION

When I was growing up, there were many misunderstandings between my dad and me. Because he had not experienced a true father in his own childhood, he did not know how to nurture his own children. I was afraid of his outbursts of anger, and I walked on eggshells for the first twenty-one years of my life. Fear was my constant companion where Dad was concerned. I grew to deeply resent him as time and again he would fly into a rage, slap me across the face, or throw me to the floor and kick me. I was filled with bitterness and jealousy when I saw how nice he treated other people. Why could he not treat me the same? I could not confront him even when I was an adult because I feared him. When I would stop by their house as an adult, my dad would go back into his study and shut the door. Who was this person who would completely change when he was around others and especially when he would enter church?

In the fall of 2001, the Lord did something way beyond my expectations that I marvel at it even now. My parents sold their home in a small town nearby. They were unable to find a suitable place to live, and my mother needed help with my dad due to his health problems. The Lord gave me a dream and showed me He wanted my parents to move into my home with me and my daughter, Sarah. Now, in my world, this was downright crazy thinking! But with God, things are completely different. His ways are so far above our human thoughts.

I felt impressed to visit my parents and present this option to them. To my surprise, they immediately agreed. God was already preparing them to live with me. Dad told me that when he came for his last haircut, he looked around at the downstairs area and gave some thought to living in this part of my home. But he had not mentioned it to my mom or to me until now.

With grit and determination, we moved ahead with our plans. The Lord began to speak to me about giving my parents the entire upstairs, including the master suite, living room, dining room, and kitchen. I was also to give up my office in the third bedroom so Dad could watch John Wayne and Fox News without driving my mom nuts. He began to call himself the "mayor of the penthouse suite." On our first Christmas together, I had a plaque made with those words, and Dad promptly hung it on the outside of the door to his TV sanctuary. I moved downstairs into my son's old bedroom with a small adjoining family room and bathroom. My salon was there as well. We settled in for our first winter, and I felt a deep sense of satisfaction in having obeyed God. There were many adjustments to make, but we all worked together, and there was contentment in my home.

One night Sarah and I went out with friends for dinner and games. We were out late and arrived home about eleven. The next morning, Dad wanted to talk to me about my *curfew*. Now, since I was in my early fifties, I told him those days were over. I did, however, agree to call them if I would be out past ten. This seemed to suit Dad. But then, about a month later, Mom and Dad went out to their friends' for the evening. It was well past ten, and they had not given me a courtesy call. At about midnight, I met them in the downstairs hallway as they tried to sneak up the steps to the penthouse. I looked at my watch and told them we would discuss their *curfew* in the morning. I was holding back the laughter as I spoke to them. Smiling sheepishly, they climbed the stairs to the penthouse. Not one word was spoken about a curfew after that night.

Dad's health took a turn for the worse. He had two heart surgeries in one month, and the prostate cancer began to invade other parts of his body. Numerous trips to the hospital and several times of prayer over him would come. We had the paramedics at the house four times in four days. One time Dad had applied too many pain patches and overdosed himself. Mom was reluctant to remove them, so I lifted up his T-shirt and ripped off two of them. I got a dirty look, but he was high as a kite and unable to respond to my tugging on the patches. Dad had slept for ten hours straight, and I knew something was wrong since it was during the day. When he tried to get up from his chair, he fell down, and we had to call the paramedics once again to lift him into bed.

Having both of my parents in such close proximity for so many years began to give me a different perspective. God brought my parents into my home for reasons only He knew. Because of my walk with God, I learned to hear His voice and recognized when He was speaking to me. It was as if I was standing on the outside of my own life. It was as if God was giving me understanding, showing me what was true about them versus what I thought was true!

One day my Mom got stung by a bee and Dad set out to spray the bees nest. He walked slowly with a cane and I knew he would get stung. He was not swayed by my opinion and went ahead with his plans. Sure enough he got more than he bargained for. Swarms of bees went after him and he had to be pulled into the dining room while I sprayed bee killer around him and Mom swatted him with the fly swatter. He got several stings and we ended up going to the emergency room with him since he had many other medical concerns. On the trip to the hospital Dad turned to Mom and said, "I'll bet you loved hitting me with that swatter didn't you?" In the backseat Sarah began to sing the honeycomb cereal song as I began to quote, "to bee or not to bee that is the question."

Through many events, the Lord revealed to me the true heart of my dad. He requested prayer from me on several occasions, and I saw a softer side of him that only the Lord knew existed. One day my dad told me he was proud of the woman I had become. I really did not know how to receive those words from him. He also told me he would like to hug my neck, except his pants would fall down if he let go of holding them up. He had become so thin. In the upstairs hallway that day, I held Dad's pants up, and he laid his head on my shoulder. I hugged him tightly, and the Lord told me to memorize the moment.

I heard the Holy Spirit speak into my thoughts, "Donna, I want you to only call me your Father. He is your dad. I used him to give life to you, but I am your Father." I thought that was very special. I felt very secure.

There were many long talks, many times of laughter with my dad. His health was rapidly declining; we had to put him in a nursing home for the final seventeen days of his life. During this time, I sang to him, read him scriptures, and massaged his legs. The Lord has given me so many great memories with my dad. He completely healed all of the pain of my past with him.

On September 7, 2007, my dad went to be with the Lord. As my sister and I sat waiting for the funeral home to come for his body, we talked about how God was with us in supernatural ways during the final days of Dad's life. I can say every stone had been upturned by the Lord, and there was nothing left within my heart to deal with regarding our relationship. I did not cry one tear for my dad. There was no hardness in my heart because there was healing and joy between us. I am so thankful for God's love toward me; He gave me a chance to be restored to my earthly dad.

PERSONAL REFLECTION

I often prayed about my attitude toward my dad for the years of hurt between us. I did not want to stand by his grave and feel there was anything left undone. When I walked out of the nursing home the night he died, my prayers were answered. As "Taps" was played at his gravesite, I did cry because of the finality of my struggles with Dad and how things had changed for the best. When God does it, He does it well!

Do not call anyone on earth your father, for
One is your Father, He who is in heaven.
—Matthew 23:9 (NKJV)

CHAPTER 56

TWO WIDOWS, AN ADVENTURE, AND A DOG

Mom and I began to adjust to a new schedule on the home front. We each attended a different church, and I was still busy in my salon. Without the busy schedule of doctor's appointments, Mom began to relax. We enjoyed outings to antique shops and second-hand stores. One of our trips included a drive to Mom's hometown of Little Rock. One day we passed by the family homestead and saw the new owners outside. We struck up a conversation with them, which led to a tour of the old house. Mom told them stories of the strange rooms they found inside—the old cellar, who built it, and why they found hundreds of copies of *National Geographic* in the attic.

We also went to the cemetery so Mom could show me where her dad was buried as well as her grandparents. My grandparents had lost a baby boy after birth due to defects in his intestinal tract. Mom never knew where baby Billy was buried, but we found his gravesite. It was a time of healing for Mom, and I could feel the presence of God with us. My grandfather's grave did not have a cross on the headstone, and this bothered Mom, so we went into Lacey and bought a stick-on cross. We returned to his grave, applied the cross, and stood on it to be sure it adhered to the stone. We returned two years later, and with all of the weather hitting it, we were surprised, but it was still there.

My brother Peter and his wife decided to move here from Alaska. We were glad they were coming to join us. Peter was a K-9 police officer and had two very well-trained dogs he brought with them. I noticed how much he loved them; he and his wife were very close to their pets.

When I was a little girl, I had a little brown puppy. Dad became angry because the dog had an accident on the floor in the kitchen. He lost his temper and threw the dog against the wall. It scared me and hurt me deeply. The next day, the dog was gone. There would be other dogs to come and go, some hit by cars, but from that point on, my young heart was stone cold about pets.

About two years after Dad died, I went to a birthday party at a friend's house, and God had a divine appointment there to heal my pet issue. My friend Nancy rescued miniature Schnauzers. I had seen many of her rescue dogs before, but this time there was this little, fuzzy, gray and white dog that caught my eye. She was in the corner and shaking from fear. She was found abandoned on a street in another city. I picked her up, and as I snuggled with her, something inside of me began to stir. I whispered to her, "Somebody is going to give you a good home, and they are going to love you so much."

I came home that evening and could not forget about this dog! I heard the voice of the Lord say to me that I was that somebody who would give this dog a good home. He said she was His provision for me and He would heal this broken place within my heart that died so long ago. I told Mom I was going to bring the dog home on trial for a couple weeks. I called my friend Nancy. She already knew that dog was for me! The process of adoption took a couple of weeks, and Nancy brought my dog, Holly, to us at Christmas, wrapped up in a blanket with red bows in her fur. I was in love! Holly was a wonderful addition to our home, and she brought comfort and love to us for almost six years. I had not really cared much about the feelings of people who lost a pet, but that all changed when I lost Holly.

So many special times came and went for Mom and me as we lived under the same roof. I became Hotel Donna to family members who would visit when they were in this area for business. All this gave me new perspectives, and I enjoyed these years with my mom. We were two widows out to enjoy adventure, and we did!

PERSONAL REFLECTION

Even the little things that hurt us are big to God. He showed me He was going to touch the tiniest detail of every petal in my life, and He definitely meant it!

Even the sparrow has found a home, And
the swallow a nest for herself,
Where she may lay her young—Even Your altars,
O Lord of hosts, My King and my God.
—Psalm 84:3 (NKJV)

CHAPTER 57

AMELIA IS COMING!

A close family friend, Peter, married while we lived in Fairbanks, Alaska. He and his wife had a sweet little baby girl named Amelia. Peter was like a big brother to me. I was an auntie now, and she was such a little doll! Being barely a teenager myself, I was busy with school schedules and making sure my hair was done just right. I did not see much of Amelia after we moved to another state. Eventually the visits with Amelia stopped.

In time, Peter's wife left him and took sweet little Amelia with her. Life moved on, and for several years when I occasionally saw Peter, he would mention trying to find his sweet daughter. He needed to know where, who, and how she was.

At this point in time, I had built my salon, and as I was working one day, I heard the Holy Spirit whisper to my mind, "Amelia is coming!" I was excited but a little hesitant because I had no idea what this would entail. I went upstairs and told my parents what I had heard, but they paid no attention to me. So I prayed and put it on the back burner. Once in a while, I felt prompted to look online for her, even searching for her name on Facebook. I was unsuccessful, but God had a plan.

Peter made an appointment with me to get his hair cut, and the Holy Spirit told me to ask his permission to search for her. It had been forty years since he had seen Amelia, and he was fearful of being rejected once again. Since he had been a police officer his "Spidey" senses were sharpened by years in law enforcement.

The day arrived for Peter's haircut, and I sensed the Lord prompting me to ask him if he trusted me. He replied, "Yes, I trust you." I told Peter what the Lord had spoken to me about Amelia, and I asked for his permission to search for her. He advised me to be careful because he did not know the response I would receive from her or her family. He began to tell me what he knew. I had no idea that he was aware of any information, but then that was the tough policeman inside of him—Mr. Investigator! I prayed over the information and asked the Lord to open up the door for me. Peter had to meet her; he needed that hole filled up. Amelia had a right to meet her father and have her emotional need met as well.

What I did not know was Amelia lived in this area, and her daughter had just told her to get on Facebook because she said, "Maybe you will find people from high school." Then the Holy Spirit said to me, "Now look on Facebook!" I went downstairs and signed into my computer, typed in her name, and there she was! I sent her a message telling her I knew her father, and if she had questions, then I probably would have answers. Amelia was also online at the same time. Her reply to me was a question, "You mean that he wants to know me?" She had been told that he had no desire to know her and had rejected her. Actually, she had been told many negative things. I gave her my phone number, and she called. She had a conversation with me and my family that day. We decided to meet Amelia, her husband, and daughter the next day.

I then called Peter. I could hear him rushing up the stairs to his office to look on Facebook. He yelled, "That's her!" The next day was my birthday, and we were having a special dinner at my house. I invited Amelia and her family to come over so she could see her father for the first time in forty years. I was overjoyed for all of us!

My daughter, Sarah, and I met the family first at their church not far from our house. We worshipped and took communion together. It was wonderful, and I was anxious for the reunion with Peter and his wife, Martha, that afternoon. Would three o'clock ever arrive? Peter kept adjusting his tie and pacing in my living room.

Another family member said to me, "Don't you think you're moving a little fast here?" But I knew what the Lord had told me. I thought that forty years was long enough. When the Jones family truck pulled up, I made my way to the front door. As I greeted them, I told Amelia her father was awaiting her upstairs in the living room. Amelia, her husband, and daughter walked up the steps. I had the sense we were being joined by a very special family. It was the most beautiful reunion! As Peter held out his arms to her, Amelia said, "Daddy," and was wrapped up in his hug. I heard him whisper into her curly dark brown hair, "I am never letting you get away again!" Amelia sat beside her daddy on the couch and said, "I know you're looking at my nose!" He denied the accusation as Amelia laughed and said she had always been told she had her father's nose. It was priceless.

I stood back watching God fulfill what He had spoken to me. Amelia had indeed come as God said she would. She came back to a family who always wanted her. It was a peaceful reunion and seemed so natural. The following years would glue Peter together with his daughter, son-in-law, and granddaughter. Questions were asked and also answered by the only one who mattered—Daddy.

Now they can move into the future. We are so thankful for God's timing and His design in bringing Amelia back to all of us. She had a right to know her father and his family.

PERSONAL REFLECTION

I believe God saw the hurt in both Peter and his daughter. His desire was to restore them. I am content knowing that void was filled, and I had the best birthday ever as I watched God fulfill what he had spoken to me. Amelia is a wonderful woman and friend. She's strong in her faith in Jesus and also anointed to minister God's love to others.

> Behold, children are a heritage from the Lord,
> The fruit of the womb is a reward.
> Like arrows in the hand of a warrior, So
> are the children of one's youth.
> —Psalm 127:3–4 (NKJV)

CHAPTER 58

WE'RE NOT THERE YET!

As I was growing up, our family went through many hardships that stirred up a lot of fear in me. We suffered the loss of all our household goods in the 1964 Great Alaska Earthquake. Then in 1968 we had a flood in Fairbanks, and the river flooded our home. Four feet of water traveled through our house, leaving destruction and several inches of mud everywhere. At the onset of the flood, my mother drove our car through about two and a half feet of rushing water as we headed out of town after midnight. I was only thirteen years old. I think I repented of every sin I could think of that night. Fear was so strong over me, and it followed me in different forms as I grew up—fear of rejection, fear of the future, fear of poverty, fear of people. The list goes on and on. Fear has more flavors than that famous ice-cream parlor!

People think, *Well, that's just life.* However, this is not God's will for the life of a Christian. Think about this ... the Bible says over 350 times in one form or another to "fear not." In 2 Timothy 1:7 (NKJV), it says, "For God has not given us a spirit of fear, but of power and of love and of a sound mind."

If God hasn't given it to us, then who did?

In 1 John 4:18 (NKJV), it says, "There is no fear in love; but perfect love casts out fear, because fear involves torment. But he who fears has not been made perfect in love."

I had developed a habit of looking at future events looming ahead on a monthly calendar and having a sense of evil foreboding about how, why, when, and what could or would happen. Every what-if in the book would pop into my thoughts. I would rehash, rewind, and think things to death. Then the Lord began to correct me. I began to stand against fear when I felt it coming on; I spoke out loud that I was not going to give any form of fear a place in my mind. I rebuked the spirit of fear and found out it would leave and peace would come. God began to show me I could either give into it or fight it.

Basically, I felt a deep impression that said, "We're not there yet! Stop living in the future!"

I made a decision to live in the moment, in the day, and not worry about anything until it was right in my face. I found most mountains really are molehills when you get right up to them. All of the *evil forebodings* that were thrown at my mind were only gutless nothings. Doesn't that make you mad when you think about it? How much sleep have we all lost because we all worried about nothing?

One of my nieces went to Thailand on a mission's trip, and a close family member was absolutely scared to death she was going to be kidnapped. I told them that the Lord was with her and Thailand was just next door to Him. I said she didn't need to worry about it. Well, that didn't go over well because she told me, "My worries have kept this family safe for over forty years!" I responded, "I thought God had done that!"

I think this scripture is a wonderful way of looking at life:

"Therefore do not worry, saying, 'What shall we eat?' or 'What shall we drink?' or 'What shall we wear?' "For after all these things the Gentiles seek. For your heavenly Father knows that you need all these things. But seek first the kingdom of God and His righteousness, and all these things shall be added to you. Therefore, do not worry about tomorrow, for tomorrow will worry about its own things. Sufficient for the day is its own trouble." (NKJV)

If you are a Christian, then Jesus knows who you are, and He knows where you live. He has already made provision for every single one of your days, so relax because we're not there yet!

PERSONAL REFLECTION

It's no wonder Jesus told us to *cast our cares on Him* and He said He would give us His peace that *surpasses all understanding.* Applying those truths to our everyday thought life is hard work. But we can do it; we must! There are many life issues regarding finances, family, work, and health, just to name a few. I do not believe Jesus left us without advice as to how we should manage our daily lives and stay in peace.

"Peace I leave with you, My peace I give to you;
not as the world gives do I give to you.
Let not your heart be troubled, neither let it be afraid."
—John 14:27 (NKJV)

Jesus still means this!

CHAPTER 59

VIETNAM VINDICATION

During my husband's service in the army, he spent a year in Vietnam. While there, he had seen the planes overhead spraying both Agent Orange and Agent White. The dioxide poison was meant to destroy the foliage so the enemy could not hide in the trees and shoot our soldiers. But it was also poisoning them.

The Veterans Administration had sent us a letter in 1983 confirming Dave had been exposed to over 250,000 gallons of the dioxide during his tour of duty. Dave died in 1990 of a disease related to the dioxide, but the VA had not yet made it a part of their service-related death list. This list would have qualified me, as his widow, to receive both financial support and medical coverage for the rest of my life. I knew the red tape with the VA was a never-ending road. I did not apply when Dave died because his disease was not on the list. I knew I would be denied, so why should I apply for benefits I knew I did not qualify for? But God was my husband, and he saw the future and wanted to provide for me.

One day the Lord led the wife of a retired VFW agent into my salon, and she became a weekly client. Ida told her husband about my husband's death and his tour in Vietnam. He kept after her to have me go talk to the Veterans of Foreign Wars. I finally went to the VFW office, and upon my arrival a very nice lady helped me navigate the red tape, and I applied for benefits. As expected, I was denied. But at least my name was in their system.

Within a couple of years, the VA announced they added the disease that killed Dave to their list of service-related diseases, and I now qualified for benefits. If I filled right away, I would receive a retroactive payment. I had to deal with more red tape and more paperwork. Then I sat back and waited two years before I heard from them. Eventually the VA gave me a lump-sum payment going back to the date I had applied at the VFW, but not to the date of Dave's death seventeen years earlier. But once again God had a plan.

My son, Martin, and his wife just happened to buy a house across the street from a man named Tim, who worked for an agency who fought for war widows to receive their proper compensation. At a neighborhood barbeque, Tim struck up a conversation with Martin about their lives, and of course Dave's death from Agent Orange was discussed. Tim asked to meet with me and review my paperwork. We met, and Tim asked us to accompany him to his Seattle office to meet with his supervisor. The meeting was short and to the point. The supervisor asked me if I had applied for and been approved for Social Security survivor benefits in 1990 when David died. Yes, I had! The supervisor raised his hands and said, "We got them!" There was a federal law that basically stated if I had applied to Social Security in 1990, this was considered the same as applying to the Veterans Administration.

In essence, the VA had to pay me retroactive death benefits for the other seventeen years! I filled out the claim once again, citing the federal law, and I sent in a copy of my Social Security approval form from 1990. It would take another year for my claim to be processed and approved. Then, there were two more times the VA made serious oversights. They only paid me for myself and did not recognize our two children. The Holy Spirit was watching the red tape, and He exposed the errors. The money was enough to pay off my mortgage, buy a car, do a few home repairs, and give my children a financial gift.

I would never have known how or when to do any of the detailed legal work by myself. God used one of my customers, my son, Martin, and Tim to reveal the issues and provide vindication to me. I went to Dave's grave and said, "They finally admitted they poisoned you, honey. It's a done deal!"

PERSONAL REFLECTION

I know who the glory goes to; it all belongs to Jesus Christ who sees to take care of all my needs! Sometimes there are no words to express the feelings of my heart. I just shake my head and smile, and whisper, "Lord, you are something else!" I think He gets my meaning.

Then Job answered the Lord and said: "I
know that You can do everything,
And that no purpose of Yours can be withheld from You."
—Job 42:1–2 (NKJV)

And my God shall supply all your need according
to His riches in glory by Christ Jesus.
—Philippians 4:19 (NKJV)

CHAPTER 60

I Saw You, Donna!

The Lord spoke something very special to me about a future husband. Needless to say, after waiting for twenty-three years, I had become hopeless and impatient for the fulfillment of this promise. I will share the details in another chapter. Human emotions get the best of us at times, and we forget that as Christians, our lives and the seasons of our lives are not in our hands, but in God's. This story will show you how personal He is with me, step by step, intricately arranging each detail for the fulfillment of His promises.

It was February 2013, and I was invited to a friend's house for a special Valentine's Day gathering. Brenda asked a handful of her closest friends to come for a luncheon at her home and to bring something for a gift exchange. The week before, I was at a local retail store known for their variety of household decorations and various other items. It is the go-to place if you want something unique at a good price. I was just browsing the aisles and saw a beautiful journal with a scripture on the front. I put it in my cart. Right across the same aisle, I saw a cute heart-shaped plate and decided to purchase it too. I began to move on when suddenly I had a change of heart. I said to myself, "What do you need with these things? You're shopping out of frustration, Donna. Get a grip!" So I put the journal and plate back on the shelf and walked away.

I continued to peruse the aisles and prayed, telling God I was tired of waiting and I was lonely and frustrated. Did He not realize how long I had been waiting for Him to fulfill what He came to me and spoke? I didn't ask for it. He was the one who told me, so could we just get on with it? I left empty-handed that day but felt relief from my emotional roller coaster through a time of prayer.

The days passed, and the Valentine's party was at hand. I was looking forward to the distraction it would provide, the taco feed, and the gift exchange. I knew each of the ladies invited with the exception of one. I will call her Ann. She was older than I was and had a strong faith in God and a prophetic gift. We sat together enjoying our tacos and began to get acquainted. After lunch, we played a few games, and Brenda handed out numbers for us to pick out a gift. All of the gift bags were decorated so nicely; you know how girls can bling things up!

My eyes were on one of the biggest bags of course, and it was gorgeously decorated. But deep inside of me, I heard this voice: "You know, Donna, it is more blessed to give than to receive. Be satisfied with less, my daughter. Pick the brown bag. Leave the others for someone else." I could not ignore the voice; I knew who had spoken to me! So, when my number came, I chose a small, plain, brown paper bag with a simple bow. When I turned to sit down, my new friend Ann said, "Donna, before you open the gift, let me tell you something." Ann began to talk, and everyone attentively listened. She said the Lord directed her to a certain store, to a certain aisle, and to two particular items. She said the Lord told her that the woman who would choose her bag needed to know He *saw* her all the time and to not give up on His promise to her so long ago.

I opened my bag to discover both the same journal and heart-shaped plate I had almost purchased the week before. I was so humbled and stunned! I began to relate to all the ladies my shopping story and almost buying those items just a few days before. God shops at Ross? Oh, wow, where can I go that He does not see me? Nowhere! ... I am so glad! The ladies gathered around me and prayed for me about the promise I was anticipating.

PERSONAL REFLECTION

Ann and I had never met before and she had no idea of my long wait. God wanted to meet me in a special way that day and he certainly did. My emotions, my impatience, and my attitude got a major overhaul at the party. It would not be long until my promise from God was fulfilled.

> Why are you cast down, O my soul? And
> why are you disquieted within me?
> Hope in God; For I shall yet praise Him, The
> help of my countenance and my God.
> —Psalm 42:11 (NKJV)

CHAPTER 61

ANOTHER LESSON ON FORGIVENESS

I asked the Lord to leave nothing unfinished in my heart as He continued to prune my life. Many things can hide in the archives of our souls. Only God knows how to dig them out and to deal with them.

Feeling resentful was something I latched onto a long time ago, and I believed I had every right to hold onto and nurse those grudges. Once I was wronged, I had a tough time letting go of it. But God's Word is clear; we must forgive others.

"Let all bitterness, wrath, anger, clamor, and evil speaking be put away from you, with all malice. And be kind to one another, tenderhearted, forgiving one another, even as God in Christ forgave you" (Ephesians 4:31–32 NKJV).

Let me give you a little example from my history.

In the late eighties, there was a woman from my church who made my life difficult. I will not use her real name to guard her privacy but only tell a little of the story of how God dealt with me about my own attitude that needed His adjustment! I don't mean to be unkind, but this woman rubbed me the wrong way! The Lord had been dealing with me about being a better homemaker. This meant keeping up with the housework, planning meals, and being a good steward of our single income. Grace would show up at my door uninvited and mock the fact that I had my housework done. She would look around and say, "I suppose you already know what your family is having for dinner too?" She would roll her eyes at me as if I had done something wrong. She would be sarcastic toward me in front of other friends at church as well.

I was homeschooling my two children while babysitting three other children for added income. My days were well planned out, and I was feeling very good about my organization and thankful for God's help in it all. I loved that I had a desire to change and become a better helpmate to Dave and a better mom to my kids. On the other hand, this lady's house was a mess, and she did not care. Her words felt like fingernails on a chalkboard when she was around me. I just wanted to tell her to stay home and clean her own house and leave me alone.

I decided to put some distance between us. After Dave died, we lost contact, and I changed churches. About five years later, I received a message online from this lady. She told me that I had been a good example to her children of a real Christian, and she thanked me for that. I was shocked and humbled because I had no idea she felt that way.

Several years later, I heard she had died. I saw online that she had come to a place in her life where she had asked God to make her a strong woman of faith. I only knew the old person she had been, and my attitude was still based on the old memories and hurtful events of the past. I saw many honorable comments about her and who she had become in the years since I had seen her. I never knew that side of her. I felt really convicted, and I regretted that I did not know her toward the end of her life. God began to show me that He is the same with all of His children who ask Him to change them. My opinion did not matter, and she did not owe me any explanation. She was accountable to God alone.

PERSONAL REFLECTION

I asked the Lord to forgive me for the longstanding judgment I
had held against this lady from my past. I forgave her for past words
and attitudes as well. The truth is that Christ was also dwelling
in her, and He was also her Savior, not just mine! My years of
resentment melted away. I am so glad God does not listen to my
opinions. He is so far above my thoughts and ways. God knew what
He was going to do in her life. I didn't.

> But the Lord said to Samuel, "Do not look at his
> appearance or at his physical stature, because I have
> refused him. For the Lord does not see as man sees;
> for man looks at the outward appearance,
> but the Lord looks at the heart."
> —1 Samuel 16:7 (NKJV)

CHAPTER 62

HANDLING OFFENSE GOD'S WAY

Sometimes people twist our words and rephrase them when they communicate them to others in order to get a response that brings them sympathy. I was misrepresented by a person I had just met. The twisting of my words by her hurt someone on our ministry team, and this person confronted me. I repeated to the team member what had really been said, and he believed me. We both pondered what we should do about it.

Now I had a choice to make concerning the lies spoken about me. The old Donna would go to her and let her have it, fire blazing out of my eyes and steam from my ears! But I knew the Lord would not be pleased with my response, and although I might *feel* justified, I would be under conviction by the Holy Spirit for the way I was handling the offense. I do not like going to the Holy Spirit woodshed. I have been taught by Him how to handle things like this. I chose to obey and wait for His timing on how and when to address the situation. I prayed and forgave her for the offense.

I saw her at my church a few times, and I knew it was better for me to remain distant. My emotions were still raw. It always bothers me when I am misunderstood. I think that is a human response we all have. And I do not like to hurt people's feelings either. Others who knew of the situation wanted me to hurry up and deal with her. But I knew it was not time and my own understanding would definitely blow it. God would show me when and how to approach it and walk it out, being led by the Holy Spirit.

Approximately six months later, the time came for me to retire as a hair stylist and to close my salon. I had several items remaining in my inventory, and I wanted to bless someone with them. In two boxes, I put hair colors, new towels, many miscellaneous products, and business supplies. The value of these items was approximately two hundred dollars. As I was contemplating who I should donate them to, I was reminded that the woman who twisted my words and at one time lied about me was a hair stylist as well.

The Holy Spirit prompted me to call her and offer them to her free of charge. That is exactly what I did. She was very surprised by my offer. She said she didn't understand why I would do this for her, considering what she had done to me. What I did not know was that she planned to open her own hair salon and was in need of supplies. God knew it! The fact that I was willing to just give them to her was a message of God's love to her through me. We talked for a while, and I told her some of my own testimony of how I had done the same thing in the past and how God had forgiven me. I forgave her, and we continued to talk about life, hair salon ownership, and single parenting. I certainly understood the struggles of being the only parent, and my heart went out to her.

I met her at a local restaurant and gave her the supplies. She had purchased a lovely planter with two peace doves and a floral arrangement as a thank you. She gave it to me, and we embraced. I knew God was starting a casual mentoring friendship between us. I felt the presence of God around us as we talked, and I knew He was pleased with both of us.

She has called me twice since then to pray with her over a difficult situation with her children and to also help her overcome her fear of opening her own business. She is a very sweet person who is learning how to cast her cares on her Lord. I can completely understand that, and we are sisters in the truest sense of the word!

This is how God wants us to handle offenses. It is completely done by the power of the Holy Spirit who indwells us.

PERSONAL REFLECTION

I love being in peace. I knew if I let myself go according to my emotions at the time of the offense, it would not be a good thing. Feelings are fickle, and I have learned by God's grace not to listen to my feelings. I chose to listen to the Holy Spirit once my human emotional rumblings ceased. I removed myself from the situation and let the dust settle, so to speak. This ability can only come from God.

Therefore, as the elect of God, holy and beloved, put on tender mercies, kindness, humility, meekness, longsuffering; bearing with one another, and forgiving one another, if anyone has a complaint against another; even as Christ forgave you, so you also must do.
—Colossians 3:12–13 (NKJV)

CHAPTER 63

JUDGE NOT, LEST YE BE JUDGED

From the time I became a Christian, I wanted to rejoice in my newfound abundant life. Even though I struggled with many deeply rooted strongholds from childhood, I still had a deep passion and desire to finish well in this life. That desire had nothing to do with material possessions; rather it had everything to do with standing before God and hearing Him say, "Well done, Donna!" This desire meant purging those strongholds; it was time to take care of this one in particular, being judgmental!

With growing up in church, I picked up a wrong attitude; I put my faith too much in people and not in God where it belonged. This continued into my adulthood. I set high expectations on Christian leaders, from the pastor of my home church to national church leaders to TV evangelists. One leader after another came up short in my eyes; some had moral failure, some had anger and pride issues. I got frustrated with many of them because they failed. In my mind, I held them to my standard, my expectation, and wanted to look up to them. I forgot that they were human and faulted like me.

I also didn't realize how desperately we all needed to vitally cling to the Lord on a continuous basis. It's not that these leaders shouldn't have led us with integrity or holiness, but we shouldn't have put them on a throne either where they did not belong. I got angry and frustrated as one after another fell from grace, so to speak. I was hurt; also embarrassed, because I had witnessed to many people and used these leaders as examples of who to watch on TV. It was wrong for me to do this. I should have pointed them to Jesus and to the Word of God.

As a result of my attitude, I had an inner wound full of anger and bitterness that the Lord wanted to open up and purge out these toxic emotions. He had done this before in many other situations, but this stronghold of being judgmental was locked up inside me like the gold in Fort Knox. I had become very guarded and untrusting with Christian leaders. I almost waited for them to disappoint me, expecting it to happen.

One night while I was recuperating from surgery, I ran across one of them on TV. I quickly advanced to the next channel only to have the Lord abruptly stop me. He said to me, "Donna, if I can forgive you of much, why will you not forgive him? You don't know the truth of his past; you only saw what the media presented, but I know the truth. I know his heart, and he has truly become a new man through the years. Turn back to that channel and watch. Look at his humility and his love for me. Stop judging him. You do not have that right." I turned the channel back. I saw in him the love of God, true humility, and a profound anointing of the Holy Spirit on his ministry. I cried as the Lord opened up my heart. I repented for the years of judgment I'd held against him and for all the church leaders who had let me down.

The truth is that we are in a fallen world surrounded by spiritual evil and enemies who know us too well. They know humankind to the core and how to set people up to fail. But God loves us, and He leads us into repentance and restoration. If I wanted that from God, I had to give it to others. They were God's business, not mine. Pointing a finger at them had only built a wall of bitterness within my own heart. As I chose to see this issue through God's eyes, I felt such a relief. I also now see the vital need to pray for our Christian leaders. They are targets of evil supernaturalism, and we are responsible for covering them in constant prayer and encouragement.

Personal Reflection

I am so thankful that God loved me enough to chastise me that night. Years before, because I was so angry with one of the ministers, I destroyed all his cassette tapes I had purchased. When God delivered me, I decided to reorder them! Now I love to listen to his music with new enjoyment. I also forgave others in Christian leadership for being human. We are only accountable to one, and that's not me! I have asked the Lord to leave nothing un-dealt with in my heart, and He heard me. "Thank You, Jesus!" The following scriptures are Jesus's own words. Read them with new eyes because His Word is always the truth.

> "Judge not, that you be not judged. For with what
> judgment you judge, you will be judged; and with the
> measure you use, it will be measured back to you.
> "And why do you look at the speck in your brother's eye, but
> do not consider the plank in your own eye? "Or how can you
> say to your brother, 'Let me remove the speck your eye';
> and look, a plank is in your own eye? "Hypocrite! First
> remove the plank from your own eye, and then you will see
> clearly to remove the speck from your brother's eye."
> —Matthew 7:1–5 (NKJV)

> "But if you do not forgive, neither will your
> Father in heaven forgive your trespasses."
> —Mark 11:26 (NKJV)

CHAPTER 64

A TWENTY-THREE-YEAR-OLD PROPHECY, FINALLY FULFILLED!

This story is so detailed; I am being very careful to not leave anything out. God's preparation began forty years before the final fulfillment. Please read slowly and with care because I do not want you to miss one detail!

It was 1974 in Juneau, Alaska, and Dave and I were at church for a Sunday evening service. A guest speaker was invited to speak. This minister had a gift of speaking prophetically over people with scriptures from the Bible regarding their future. He called me to the front. I went but was reluctant to receive his ministry. He spoke several scriptures to me, and I was given a copy of them. It scared me because at that time I still viewed God as angry and vengeful, so I threw out the paper with the scriptures. But a woman at the church was making copies of each person's list of scriptures. Little did I know her copies would be in a box kept safely in her attic for the next eighteen years.

We had moved to Washington State in 1983. One morning when I was in the shower, I began praying about my marriage to Dave. We had grown apart, and I could feel it. Something was bothering me, and I felt the need to get alone with God and talk to Him. As I prayed, I became aware of God's sweet presence. The following message came loudly into my spirit, almost like a lightning bolt of power: "One day your sister will introduce you to your future husband." Now I knew God's voice, but I could not make sense out of what He had just spoken to my spirit. My husband was asleep in the other room. I was simply puzzled; the words were strange to me. Within a month, I had put it on the back burner of my mind, and life went on.

In an earlier chapter, "The Darkest Valley," I shared with you the story of Dave's death. After about eighteen months of grieving for him, on a lonely Sunday afternoon I began to pray, "Lord I don't want to grow old all by myself." Then softly I heard in my spirit, "Remember what I spoke to you in the shower that night, Donna. One day your sister will introduce you to your future husband." God had all of my attention at that moment, and I was more than overwhelmed when I cried out, "Oh, Jesus! That really was You! Oh, Lord, You have to confirm this through your Word. I need to hear from You about this!"

I waited two weeks for confirmation and heard nothing. Then one day, when it was God's timing, the phone rang. It was my mother-in-law, Ruth, in Juneau. She said to me, "Donna, do you remember back in 1974 at church there was a minister who gave you scriptures over your life?" I told her yes I did remember, and it scared me. She asked me if I still had my copy of the scriptures, and I told her no. Ruth said, "Well, the lady who made copies of the scriptures had a house fire. In the attic was a box that was not burned in the fire. In that box was a list of scriptures with your name on it. Would you like me to send it to you?" I said I would love to have them, not thinking that these scriptures would be the confirmation regarding the future marriage. When they arrived in the mail, I looked them all up. Most of the scriptures were on wisdom and the knowledge of God's Word. But the last scripture on the list was from Isaiah 34:16 (NKJV),

"Search from the book of the Lord, and read: Not one of these shall fail; Not one shall lack her mate. For My mouth has commanded it, and His Spirit has gathered them."

I researched this scripture further. Basically, it is about prophecy that God has spoken and He will bring its fulfillment. I read and reread each of the scriptures. I am so thankful the box was protected in that attic by the Lord and did not burn in the fire.

Now I have one blood sister, and she lived in another state. I had no desire to relocate there and wondered how I would ever meet someone through her. But as usual, God's ways are not my ways, and I am so glad! I would have to wait for twenty-three years before my 'sister' would introduce me to this husband. I had no idea there were other events I needed to walk through to learn the things God had to teach me before the fulfillment of this prophecy.

People have asked me why God would speak to me about a future husband before Dave's death. God is the author of life itself. He has prophesied over His people since the beginning of time, so why wouldn't He? I did not have any fear when He spoke to me in the shower that night. I don't try to understand God and why He chooses to do things the way He does. He is God! But I was wondering daily, always waiting and trying to figure out what and how this would all be fulfilled. There were many times I needed a man around the house, someone to help me with my children and decisions that needed to be made.

My sister would call me on occasion for general conversation, and my heart would skip a beat when I heard her voice. She called me once to tell me she had some pictures to give to me. She would somehow find a way to send them. As I sat thinking about it early one morning, I began to reason out the answer. I thought, *Maybe she's going to meet a man who is visiting California, and maybe he will bring them to me, and just maybe he will be the one God told me about.*

As soon as I began thinking on this scenario, I suddenly

perceived in my spirit loud laughing that seemed to be coming from above me on the right side. Then I heard, "You and your tiny mind trying to figure God out!" Then He said this: "Don't you know that anything your human mind can figure out would never be how God does it?" It took me by surprise, and I began to laugh myself. Doubt would try to press in on me, but I knew what God had said to me. I could not and would not deny it.

I told a close friend at church about my prophecy, and she believed it too. About a year later, a friend of her family moved to Washington. He was a former pastor who was divorced (I will call him James). I was being very careful to guard myself from false suitors, and yet I did not want to miss out on God's will either. James began to pursue me at church, and I noticed some things about him that bothered me.

He kept asking me how much money Dave had left me and said he could help me invest it. Okay here is red flag #1. He sat behind me in choir and kept trying to tell me off-color jokes. Okay here is red flag #2. He also asked me how old my daughter was, and when I replied she was fourteen, he said, "Well, she's almost done." Sarah was not a pie in the oven, and she and I would never be done in our relationship as mother and daughter. Okay red flag #3. Strike 3, and you are out!

James had two pre-teen children who moved to Washington with him, and they needed him more now since his divorce. He was not nurturing to them, and they both began to make some dangerous life choices. Meanwhile, I let James know that I was not interested in him other than as a casual friend. He began to look elsewhere. Within a month, James found someone else. They would be married quickly and also divorced quickly due to some child abuse issues on both sides. James moved on to date a woman who had left a gay relationship to be with him. He was found dead several months later in his motorhome, which was full of pornography.

"Thank You, Jesus, for red flags!"

God began speaking to one of the senior ladies at my church. He told Sheila He wanted her to form a special group of four ladies as a support group. She was to call this group "tea ladies." He told her one of the four ladies would be the central person that the other three would surround and pray for because a trial was coming into her life. I was this person. I met with the tea ladies several times, and the Lord put it on their hearts to cover me in prayer.

There would be another false suitor who would come into my life. Before this occurred, I had yet another encounter with God. He gave me a vision of a tall man standing facing me, and the shadow of a woman passed between us. I knew during the vision that this man and I were in a relationship and another woman was secretly in the picture. I was taken back by the vision because I was so careful to guard myself about meeting anyone. I will refer to the other woman as 'shadow woman'.

But I knew I was to meet the real person at some point. Many people were telling me that any sister in Christ could be the person God meant would do the introduction. I met the second suitor through a friend, and I will call him Frank. He seemed to be a nice man, but inside my soul I continued to find a resistance. One day I clearly heard these words: "He is the man I warned you about." I also heard, "If this was My hand, you would not feel such anxiety."

It took an encounter with the *shadow woman* to reveal the truth about Frank. As I was praying once again early in the morning, my phone rang. It was shadow woman. She said to me, "Donna, I really did not want to like you, but I do like you, and you need to know the truth." I told her that I knew the truth of their affair; the Lord had showed me. She gasped and dropped her phone. She began to cry as I also told her that I was going to get away from him. She said we made a good couple and she was going to be the one to leave because Frank was in love with me and not her.

My heart went out to shadow woman because she had been

used by Frank for almost four years. I was repulsed by his pretense and kept remembering how accurate God was in what He had shown me in the vision before I met him. I decided to go meet her in person, take her to breakfast, and pray with her. I gave shadow woman a devotional that had meant so much to me. She had recently become a Christian, and my responsibility to her was one of love, understanding, and counsel. I truly meant the words I spoke to her that day.

The Lord directed me to go down to the waterfront where I had declared that angry vow so many years before. He had shown me over time when I had vowed to move back to my hometown in 1972, it pulled my emotions and had to be broken by an act of my will and prayer. I wrote a letter asking God to forgive me for trying to manipulate my life when I had already given it to Him! I chose to submit to God's will and embrace His destiny for me. I was going to burn the letter and bury the ashes in the sand. The wind kept blowing out my matches. I went down to the corner store for a lighter, but by the time I returned, the torn-up letter was washed away by the incoming tide. That vow was completely broken, and to this day it has not pulled on my emotions again.

After God had spoken to me about my future, how could I have fallen into such a trap? Lying on my couch that night, brokenhearted, I prayed again and asked my Lord, my faithful Jesus, to forgive me and to heal my wounded heart. I had been impatient and ran ahead of Him, and I was to blame. The next day, I got a call from Sheila, my "tea lady." She said the Lord gave her a scripture for me. This is the scripture: "The voice of joy and the voice of gladness, the voice of the bridegroom and the voice of the bride, the voice of those who will say: 'Praise the Lord of hosts, For the Lord is good, For His mercy endures forever'" (Jeremiah 33:11 NKJV). What a perfect scripture for me and right on time! Yes, the voice of joy and the voice of the bridegroom and bride would be heard once again in my life!

Sheila moved out of state before the whole Frank drama finished out its course, and she had no idea what had happened. The Lord whispered to her heart, "Remember Bud." Sheila never told me what name God whispered to her, but she continued to pray for me as she settled into her new home far away.

That night I had a dream of a wedding. I saw a long aisle leading up to a man. His stature was one of confidence and also strength in the Lord. I did not see his face. In the dream, I heard this message: "Just as the first vision was fulfilled of the false suitor, so this dream will be fulfilled as well."

After the Frank drama, which lasted approximately eighteen months, I was determined to build a high wall around my emotions. I told people it would take seven trumpet blasts and four angelic visitations before I allowed myself any relationship with a man.

Another friend, named Theresa, was given a book called *Waiting on God* by Andrew Murray, who died in 1917. I had never heard of this great man of God. Theresa said the Lord spoke to her that the book was for me, not her. I graciously accepted it and began to read. I read it every day, month after month, for five years. The Lord was digging up my heart once again, and I felt like I was undergoing a spiritual overhaul.

At the same time, I found a book called *God Is a Matchmaker* by Derek Prince. This book was the story of how God supernaturally matched Derek to both of his wives. His first wife was approximately twenty-three years older than he, and when she passed away, he married again. The second wife was approximately twenty years younger. Both women were chosen by God to be exactly what he needed for each season of his life as a missionary to Israel. I was struck by how closely God detailed Derek Prince's life I didn't know anyone else in my circle of friends who had such a detailed, carefully protected assignment on their lives.

I was in a bubble of God's design. I could not talk to my

extended family about any of this because they were not involved with me and it would seem strange to them. I did not want anyone to mock what I knew to be true. Rather than share, I now decided it was best to kept this tucked in my heart and wait on God. I would only tell a few select friends who believed me and prayed for me. It seemed every time my emotions were weary with waiting, I would have someone randomly say to me, "Did you know you're going to remarry?" I heard comments like this many times over. All of these were from prophetically gifted people attending my church. I finally told one girl, "Yes, you can come to my wedding someday, but I have to meet him first!" She looked a bit puzzled.

Oh, there were many times when I wished God had not told me anything about a future husband. I grew impatient and really tired of waiting. One day I angrily said to the Lord, "Do you know how long eighteen years is to a human woman?" I clearly heard Him say, "No, Donna, why don't *you* tell *Me*! I am only God Almighty!" The Lord had corrected me, and I was silent at His words.

The next Sunday at church, I was to help on a prayer team. I had my name tag on and was ready to minister at the end of the service. My pastor's teaching was on Abraham's long wait for the birth of Isaac. He talked about how hard it is to wait for a promise from God. Well, hello! I could certainly understand that subject.

My pastor ended his teaching by saying that the Lord told him there were people in the church today waiting for the fulfillment of a prophetic word the Lord had spoken to them, and some were in the second decade of waiting. That was enough for my tears to fall. I was one of those people, and I clearly felt the Holy Spirit prompt me to not pray for anyone today; rather I was to receive prayer myself. I took off my name tag and got in line.

The couple that prayed for me did not know me personally. I sat down, and the lady looked at me and said, "The Lord just told me that you were going to do great and mighty things beside your husband one day, but aren't you a widow, Donna?" That was enough to open up the gates of my emotions as I told this couple all about the prophecy spoken years before and how long I had waited already. The couple sat there in awe as I unfolded my story, detail by detail. Tom, the husband, said, "Wow, we've never heard of anything like this before!"

Then they began to pray for me. Tom said he saw a picture of a treasure chest in his mind as he prayed and that I was this treasure chest. He said the enemy, Satan, was lying to my mind, telling me no man would ever want me. He said he saw a man open up the chest and pull out pearls, diamonds, and rubies. Tom said my future husband was going to see me as a treasure. The couple was as thrilled as I was because they had heard from the Lord so clearly and Tom had his first vision! This prayer time was amazing. I went into the ladies' room afterward; I had cried all of my makeup off, but I felt great! I will never forget this time of encouragement and what a gift it was for me.

Remembering one of the things God told me was that my sister would introduce me to my future husband. But, in God's way of thinking, I had many sisters. I had been told by the tea ladies the same thing, but I was not ready to hear it. Every woman who is part of God's family is my sister!

Coming to my salon, I had many ladies who were my sisters in the Lord, and they all continued to pray for me and encourage me. One of these sisters was Lois, a client and a friend who had been talking to me about a ministry in town where she and her sister received much encouragement and healing. I would fix Lois's hair and listen to her but never went with her to this ministry. One day, Lois brought me a four-inch stack of teaching CDs from Flames of Fire Ministry. Before she left the salon, Lois looked at me and said, "Donna, you might just meet your husband there."

I didn't want to hurt Lois's feelings, and since she had brought them to me, I thought I would at least listen to one of them. Because my former church, Clover Creek Bible Fellowship, had moved into Tacoma, I was now looking for a new church home. I wanted more of the same faith-filled excitement from God. I did not want to just sit in a pew again or sing in a choir. I listened to one of Lois's teaching CDs and loved it. I also shared it with my daughter, and we decided to visit Flames of Fire Ministry that coming Friday evening.

From the moment we entered the building, we felt the presence of God. It was a comfort to me. The teaching was wonderful—biblically sound and strong. The Lord spoke to my heart and said, "You're home." For the first month, I went to both the Tuesday morning and Friday evening services. I watched and listened carefully to what was being taught. They were teaching biblical truth. I asked God to confirm to me if I was to become part of this ministry, and He answered me in His usual flair through the following events.

For about three weeks, I was reading some prophetic books, and my eyes fell on a sentence that went something like this, "… and they will be as Flames of Fire." And then again on the next three pages, the same phrase was repeated. This is found in Hebrews 1:7 and Psalm 104:4: "And concerning the angels He says, 'Who makes His angels winds, and His ministering servants flames of fire' [to do His bidding]" (AMP). The Lord kept putting the name of this ministry in front of me several times over the following week. I received one confirmation after another. I started attending Flames of Fire Ministry in Tacoma twice each week. I was hungry to learn more about God's power to "save, heal, and deliver."

I had seen healing and deliverance at Clover Creek and knew the truth of it in scripture but had never seen it so powerfully ministered as I was witnessing here at Flames of Fire. No fanfare, no money begging, just the pure power and love of God to the hurting. I kept my Bible on my lap as I was being taught, looking up every scripture as I listened carefully.

My decision to make this ministry my church home did not go unopposed. Someone I knew tried to investigate the ministry. They came up empty-handed. I was not thrilled at their choice to invade my privacy and challenge my right to follow Gods direction. Again I saw that just because God confirms something to me doesn't mean He will confirm it to others in my life. I must follow Gods direction. For Scriptures on this see: Luke 14: 26-35 (AMP)

After attending here for a couple of weeks, I decided to go forward for prayer. Pastor Gene came over to meet me, and we talked for a while. I told him what was happening in my life, and he told me to come forward to the altar for prayer. The love of God, expressed through the ministry team, was precious that evening, and the freedom I received through prayer was refreshing.

The next week, at the Tuesday morning service, I asked for prayer again. The team was composed of a man who was in his late sixties and a lady who was in her fifties. They had me keep my eyes open[5] as they asked the Lord how to minister to me. I was very exhausted by the previous years' events—widowhood, single parenting, Dad's death, church drama, and other stressful events. I didn't even know how to put it into words. The tears fell as I just stood there. I remember saying that I just wanted to finish my life well for my walk with God. My eyes were on eternity and I did not want to be distracted from what God had for my future. I had tasted and I had seen that the Lord was good indeed and I wanted more of him!

My daughter-in-law came to the ministry on her own several

---

[5] The eyes are the window to the soul; keeping them open during personal ministry can reveal the inner spiritual condition of the person receiving prayer. "The lamp of the body is the eye. Therefore, when your eye is good, your whole body also is full of light. But when your eye is bad, your body also is full of darkness" (Luke 11:34 NKJV).

times, and she returned home and told Martin, "I just met your mom's future husband." They did not tell me this until later.

I was next for prayer with Pastor Bud. JoAnne, one of the team ladies, asked me to look in the eyes of Pastor Bud as I received prayer. As I did, I saw the most loving, gentle, and kind presence of Jesus reflected in his face. The love of God poured out from Bud, and after I sat down, I remember thinking to myself, *Wow, I wonder if that's the kind of man God has for me.* After a few weeks, Pastor Gene asked me to join the ministry team. He put me with Bud, and as I was being trained, we worked very well together.

God began to work His plan. I would know what Bud was going to speak before he said a word. The Lord told me to "listen to him and obey his instructions". I heard God say that to me just in time for Bud to tap me on the shoulder. It was almost as if we were twins in so many ways—attitudes and desires for the Lord.

We went on a ministry trip to another part of our state. Bud drove my car with two other women accompanying us. I had to move into the backseat because it was way too comfortable sitting beside him. I was being extremely guarded! I later learned Bud was divorced for several years and did not have any desire to remarry. He and his wife had a son who was suddenly killed, and the marriage did not survive the tragedy.

Bud and I became good friends and had long talks about life and spiritual things. He was just as guarded as I was. There was never a hand held or dating between us. But we were both feeling a strong spiritual attraction for each other. He would tell me I was by far the strongest Christian woman he had ever met. He told God in 2002 that if He had someone for him, then He would have to "put her in my face" because he was not looking for a wife. God was indeed putting me right in his face, several times every week.

Bud had long lost any desire for another marriage; he only wanted a relationship with Jesus. As we talked, I learned that when

I was helping to feed the hungry, he was just across town doing the very same thing at his church. I also learned we were at the same concerts and Christian conferences on the same dates. Unknown to me, I had customers in my salon who were his personal friends.

About eighteen months earlier, Bud went to the ocean to relax and spend time in prayer. As he sat in his car, he saw clouds and a large stairway. He saw two angels holding swords upside down poised at attention. As he was looking at this vision, he saw a deep, plush, brilliantly green area. The next morning, a friend called Bud and said she had a dream at 3:00 a.m. that he had gotten married. Another friend had a dream of two big angels around him and a picture of a wedding. And if that's not crazy enough, several times I visited friends who were just down the block from his apartment! God must've smiled many times as I was waiting for Bud because I often drove right by his home over the years. But again, God's timing is perfect, and neither one of us were ready for the calling God had for us as a couple.

One of the women from the ministry was JoAnne, and she and I became good friends. She was a true sister in Christ. She has a very strong gift of discerning from the Lord. She began to ask me if I would be interested in Bud pursuing me. She said she saw something between us. I told her my story, but she still believed God had shown her that Bud and I were to be married. I told JoAnne to leave it alone and let God be in charge. I also told her that after being pursued by other false suitors, it would take an act of God before I would let any man get that close to me again. I had to see God at work and have Him prove it beyond any doubt.

Not long after this, Bud offered to take JoAnne and me to the gun range to practice shooting. We wanted to improve our gun-handling skills. We had the best time, and of course the three of us went out to dinner afterward. My son, Martin, called me and said he and his wife believed Bud was to be my husband and I needed to stop being fearful. I told him since he had called me, he should pray for me right then. Boy, did he ever pray!

One day, the Lord told JoAnne she was not to go shooting with us. He told her He needed to draw Bud and me together and she was in the way. JoAnne called me and told me this tidbit of information. We were nervous to be alone together at the gun range, but when we went to dinner, it was six solid hours of conversation. It seemed like only two. The waitress kept our water glasses full as we talked on and on and on. Bud smiled at me and said that he could have talked to me for another six hours.

A few weeks later, Bud called me and said he realized we had grown closer than he intended and he liked his life as it was. He wanted to be friends, but there was no future marriage coming for him. I went outside to cut firewood, a lot of firewood! I was partly relieved and partly confused. I felt a strong bond forming between us, and I knew if he was not the one, then I had to get away from him. I could not have such a strong tie of friendship to anyone but the one God had been telling me about. Of course, that meant I'd leave Flames of Fire because it would be too hard to stay there.

Bud was exactly the image in the second wedding aisle dream God had given to me. I did not understand it, but at the same time, it was twenty-three years of waiting, and I had been wrong before. I decided to get away from Bud and from the ministry where he was associate pastor. I tried to figure out how to leave. I knew I was getting older, but I also knew at some point God would fulfill what He had spoken over and over again.

Within a few days, Bud called me again. It was a Saturday afternoon, and he wanted to talk about some details of a ministry time from the prior evening. Bud asked me if I'd had dinner yet, and since it was only 4:00 p.m., I had not eaten. We decided to meet at a Chinese restaurant in town. As we ate, we talked. It was a pleasant conversation, more history of our lives ... no stress, no big expectation. Bud began to tell me his opinion of something, and silently I prayed. "Okay, God, enough already! If he is the man you have for me, then this has to get going, or I am done!"

Suddenly, Bud put his hand up to his eye and said, "The Lord is talking to me." In my mind, I said, "Wow, God, that was fast!" Then I heard Bud say, "Oh no!" I asked him if we needed to leave, and he said, "Yes, we do." God had said the word *marriage* to Bud's mind and also, "You asked me to put your wife in your face. Donna is your wife." At first I was taken back and bewildered when he said, "Oh no!". The truth is that Bud had become contented as a single man. God had drawn us together in a strong spiritual tie that He grew within us without our realizing it. Bud had given up on finding the right person. But God had a surprise for him and was about to rearrange his life in a big way.

So we went to our local park where Bud asked me, "Is there is anything more in your heart toward me than just friendship?" I turned my head away to look out the car window. The moment I had waited for was right in front of me. I wanted to run and to stay at the same time. Bud said to me, "Look me in the eyes."

With tears running down my face, I said, "I told you what the Lord spoke to me long ago."

He then said to me, "I was doing just fine, and then you showed up and messed me up good! I love Gene and the ministry team, but girl, God has given me an overwhelming *love* for you! God poured out a supernatural love over me in the restaurant when I heard the word *marriage* and that I am to take care of you and guard you for the calling on our life together." Bud realized it was not a request of God that we marry; it was a [6]mandate. It felt good, and it felt right

---

[6] Mandate means that God has a preordained plan and purpose for this union. It is under God's authority, not humankind's determination.

to both of us. Then he took my hand in his and said, "Donna, I am going to be your husband. You have a [7]covering."

The car was filled with laughter, joy, tears, and the presence of God. We decided he should talk to Gene, the senior pastor at Flames of Fire, and get his blessing. He set up the meeting right away, and Gene told him God had shown him I was to be Bud's wife eighteen months earlier, and he was told by God to keep quiet and watch. We called my daughter, Sarah, and she cried with joy! She had become friends with Bud on the worship team and was hoping he would be her "God dad." My son and his wife were so glad we finally saw the light! I called my tea lady friend, Sheila, and broke the news that the prophecy was finally fulfilled. She asked for his name, and I told her it was Bud. She giggled with joy because God had told her several years before to "Remember Bud."

We broke the news at Flames of Fire Ministry, only to learn that most of the ministry team already knew what was coming. The Lord had revealed to them that we were to be married and they were to be quiet and pray! Bud also broke the news to his family, and it really surprised them, since he had said nothing until we became engaged. We began to manage decisions that had to be made regarding our living arrangements. I realized both of us were settled in our lives and knew that to get married meant many adjustments. There was so much to consider since each of us had been single for over twenty years. My Mom decided to go live with my youngest brother, and we began the fun of putting two households together.

The Lord prompted us to go to the graves of both my husband, Dave, and Bud's son, Don. It was amazing they were buried only a few steps apart from each other. We both shed many tears as we stood side by side saying our final goodbyes to the past. There was

---

[7] Covering in this context means to protect and to guard with love.

deep sense of freedom happening as sorrow lifted off both of us at the cemetery.

Friends gave me the best bridal shower; over sixty people came to wish me well. I felt very blessed as God managed every detail of our engagement and wedding. Each part was perfectly done by friends who love us. The décor and the flowers were so beautiful. Even a video and photographs were a gift from people who knew and loved us. It was a precious move of God.

July 13, 2013, we were married. Our wedding day was filled with joy and laughter. The church was packed with friends who had walked with both of us for years. Dave's sister came from Juneau as well as other friends who drove several hours to share this occasion. Family filled up the front row and watched as I shared vows with my promised husband, Bud. And JoAnne, who had known what was coming, sat watching with a big smile on her face.

When we were pronounced husband and wife, we were given a standing ovation! We felt the presence of the Lord as He confirmed over and over that we were in His will. This was the fulfillment of a promise made twenty-three years earlier.

PERSONAL REFLECTION

In God's perfect design, the marriage between Bud and me was all about unity and companionship. It is amazing how much alike we are. He is strong where I am weak, and I am strong to hold up a weaker area in him. Bud affirms me over and over again as I grow and learn more about the kingdom of God. We have a marriage completely secured in the will of God. We know each other's thoughts, feelings, and opinions and have a solid commitment to each other and to the purpose God has for us as we minister together as a couple.

I describe the ministry we are involved with as a "spiritual medical unit" for the body of Christ. We are here to lead people to a relationship with Jesus Christ and also to bring deliverance and healing to those who are in need. Christians are people who have been forgiven for their sins. But that is just the beginning. There is so much work to be done in us to bring our lives into God's original design and plan. Our true identity as His children living in His kingdom is for today, not only the future.

Humans are stubborn, and it takes time for us to realize that God truly loves us. We can trust Him as He does His miraculous works in us. Bud and I team-teach sometimes, and we have become spiritual grandparents to many. What a blessing it is for us to share this as one heart!

I want to close out this special chapter with one of the scriptures in the box that survived the fire in the attic in Juneau, Alaska, so long ago.

> Oh, what a wonderful God we have! How great
> are his wisdom and knowledge and riches!
> How impossible it is for us to understand
> his decisions and his methods!
> For who among us can know the mind of the Lord?
> Who knows enough to be his counselor and guide?
> —Romans 11:33–34 (TLB)

Bud and Donna on wedding day

Sarah and her God dad

CHAPTER 65

SOME FINAL THOUGHTS

All of the stories I have shared with you happened over a thirty-eight-year period. Most of my life I was busy with normal day-to-day activities. God knows all that, and yet He chose to interrupt my life and weave it intricately with His *details*. I love how He has done that for me. "Indeed, He had spoken it, and He also brought it to pass." I am a changed woman!

I can remember sitting in church as a child, wanting a testimony in the worst way, and God heard me even then. That memory is so clear to me now even though it took place over fifty five years ago. After many years of doing church activity, I still had no idea who He really was. I was full of unbelief and very impatient.

He was not my Santa Claus. It was never all about me; it was always about Him! "And He will do all His pleasure." Now, with great joy, I have a life of wonderful testimonies proclaiming His glory. No pit is so deep that Gods love is not deeper still. "And they overcame him by the blood of the Lamb and by the word of their testimony, and they did not love their lives to the death" (Revelation 12:11 NKJV).

Looking back to when I was in the movie theater watching *Across the Great Divide* and God spoke so clearly to me, I thought everyone there also heard Him. It seemed audible, but it was only audible to every cell of my being. His words to me once again were, "Donna, there are many things we need to change about you." My response was, "Yes, Lord, one thing at time, one day at a time." And He said, "Okay."

I can honestly say that I would not alter one thing He has required of me or taken me through. God has never made one mistake in my life, ever! He has been 100 percent faithful even when I have failed Him. Changes came, a little at a time, each one bringing forth a sweet fragrance to His glory.

Unlike human beings, when God says something, He means it, and He fulfills it!

As I close this book, dear reader, I must ask, do you truly know Jesus as Savior and Lord? Or do you only know church activity? Jesus Christ is as close as your breath, and He knows you more intimately than you can know yourself. I encourage you to reach out to Him in prayer. He will answer you! He is waiting for you to call on Him. You are the reason He came to earth and why He died on the cross—in order to pay your sin debt in full.

Pray this prayer from your heart: "Heavenly Father, I believe that You loved me so much that you gave Your only Son to die for my sin. He shed His blood on the cross just for me. I repent of all of the sins of my past, and I receive Your forgiveness. I confess that Jesus is my Savior and my Lord. I believe in my heart that God has raised Him from the dead. I am now His child, and I turn all of my life over to Him today."

> For God so loved the world that He gave His
> only begotten Son, that whoever believes in Him
> should not perish but have everlasting life.
> —John 3:16 (NKJV)

I will never forget what God said to me in that grocery store so long ago. "Drink deeply of the scent of this orange carnation. Do you see how I have detailed each petal to fit inside the other? I am going to detail your life as I have detailed this flower, and the scent of your testimony will be a sweet-smelling fragrance to My nostrils."

This has been evident through every single experience and lesson I have learned over the years. They have become a rich storehouse for me to draw on as I pray with and minister to others.

I am thankful for the many painful lessons, the funny lessons, and yes, the long periods of waiting. It all taught me so very much. I have asked the Lord to use every chapter to bring glory to His name and to help others. I hope my testimony has been a blessing you.

God's richest blessings!

Donna Gurth Hopper
August 2017

Contact Donna Hopper at: Personal Touch Outreach
                                     PO Box 4176
                                     Spanaway, WA 98387

E-mail: dhopperpersonaltouchoutreach@gmail.com

Join me on Facebook at: The Scent of My Testimony

Printed in the United States
By Bookmasters

Printed in the United States
By Bookmasters